GOD IS NEAR US

JOSEPH CARDINAL RATZINGER

GOD IS NEAR US

The Eucharist, the Heart of Life

Edited by
Stephan Otto Horn and Vinzenz Pfnür

Translated by
Henry Taylor

IGNATIUS PRESS　SAN FRANCISCO

Title of the German original:
Gott ist uns nah. Eucharistie: Mitte des Lebens
© 2001 Sankt Ulrich Verlag, Augsburg

Cover art:
Juan de Juanes (1510–1588)
The Last Supper (detail)
Museo del Prado, Madrid, Spain
Scala/Art Resource, New York

Cover design by Roxanne Mei Lum

Contents

Introduction

From the beginning, the Eucharist has held a special place in the theology of Joseph Ratzinger. In particular, it has been determinative for his understanding of the Church. "The Church originates, and has her continuing existence, in the Lord's communicating himself to men, entering into communion with them, and thus bringing them into communion with one another. The Church is the Lord's communion with us, which at the same time brings about the true communication of men with one another." [1] As the epigraph for his dissertation, *People of God and House of God in Augustine's Doctrine of the Church*, Joseph Ratzinger had already chosen: *Unus panis unum corpus sumus multi*—"We who are many are one body, for we all partake of the one bread."

Looking at this understanding of Eucharist and Church, we see a continuous and unbroken line of development from the time before the Council up to the present day, as Joseph Ratzinger's publications and addresses bear witness. This eucharistic ecclesiology even found its way into the texts of the Council.

The great value he places on traditional eucharistic piety, expressed in processions, devotional services, silent adoration before the Holy Sacrament—something to be found in this present volume, as elsewhere—is not, in the case of Joseph Ratzinger, an unexamined survival from the time before the

[1] Joseph Cardinal Ratzinger, "Gemeinde aus der Eucharistie" [Congregation from the Eucharist], in Joseph Cardinal Ratzinger, *Vom Wiederauffinden der Mitte. Grundorientierungen. Texte aus vier Jahrzehnten* [Rediscovering the heart of things. Basic directions. Texts from four decades], edited by his students (Freiburg, 1997), p. 35.

Council. It is rather the case that the significance of these forms of piety, as expressing a personal communication with Christ, has gradually unfolded for him with the passage of time.

Communion presupposes an understanding of God in which the Absolute Being is not an impersonal universal law; rather, he is word, meaning, and love, living fellowship.[2] So what is here expounded concerning the Eucharist is set within a framework of two pieces that illuminate a wider horizon: God the Trinity comes to meet us, becomes a God who is with us and among us, and this implies at the same time that at the end we do not just pass on into emptiness but find everlasting happiness in God's presence.

The great majority of the pieces on the theme of the Eucharist that have been brought together here are transcripts of tape-recorded sermons delivered in particular situations and for special occasions. We have deliberately retained this flavor of the spoken word. Nonetheless, we see the texts we have chosen as giving a new and significant impulse toward a more profound understanding of the mystery of God's intimate presence in the Eucharist.

We would like first of all to thank the author for having tirelessly, and with a commitment often extending to the limit of what is humanly possible, put himself in the service of communicating and unfolding for people the message of the Christian faith.

We would further like to thank the public relations office of the archdiocese of Munich for its friendly help in letting us see the sermons that Joseph Cardinal Ratzinger preached during his time at Munich and also Herr Helmuth Brandner for his ready help and support.

[2] Cf. ibid., pp. 17–24.

Our thanks are due to the publisher Erich Wewel Verlag for permission to reprint the four sermons published in 1978 under the title *Eucharistie—Mitte der Kirche* (Eucharist—Heart of the Church).

Not least we would like to thank the Saint Ulrich Verlag, at whose initiative this present little book was produced. Our thanks are especially due to the editor, Michael Widmann, who made available an extensive collection of sermons by Cardinal Ratzinger and who took responsibility for getting the book ready for print, and likewise to Anja Beck for her committed work in typesetting and layout.

The Editors

God with Us
and God among Us

"By the power of the Holy Spirit
He was born of the Virgin Mary, and became Man"

Like all the great creeds of the early Church, the Nicene
Creed has the basic structure of a profession of faith in the
triune God. Its essential character is that of saying Yes to the
living God as our Lord, the God from whom we have life and
to whom our life returns. It is a declaration of faith in God.
But what does it mean when we call this God a living God?
It means that this God is not a conclusion we have reached by
thinking, which we now offer to others in the certainty of
our own perception and understanding; if it were just a matter of that, then this God would never be more than a human
idea, and any attempt to turn to him could well be a reaching
out in hope and expectation but would still lead us into
vagueness. When we talk of the living God, it means: This
God shows himself to us; he looks out from eternity into
time and puts himself into relationship with us. We cannot
define him in whatever way we like. He has "defined" himself and stands now before us as our Lord, over us and in our
midst. This self-revelation of God, by virtue of which he is
not our conception but our Lord, rightly stands, therefore, in
the center of our Creed: a profession of faith in the story of
God in the midst of human history does not constitute an

exception to the simplicity of our profession of faith in God
but is the essential condition at its heart. That is why the heart
of all our creeds is our Yes to Jesus Christ: "By the power
of the Holy Spirit he was born of the Virgin Mary." We
genuflect at this clause, because at this point the heavens, the
veil behind which God is secluded, are swept aside, and the
mystery touches us directly. *The distant God becomes our God,
becomes "Emmanuel"*—*"God with us"* (Mt 1:23). The great
masters of church music have found ever new ways of making
this sentence sound out, beyond anything that can be said in
words, in such a way that the inexpressible reaches our ears
and touches our hearts. Such compositions are an "exegesis"
of the mystery more profound than any of our rational inter-
pretations. But because it was the Word that became flesh, we
must ever again strive, nonetheless, to translate into our human words this first creative Word, which "was with God"
and which "is God" (Jn 1:1), so that in those words we may
hear *the* Word.

1. Grammar and Content in the
   Sentence from the Creed

If we look at the sentence first of all according to its gram-
matical structure, we see that it talks about four agents. It
makes specific mention of the Holy Spirit and the Virgin
Mary. But then there is also the "he", of "he was born". This
"he" has previously been given various names: Christ, "the
only Son of God, . . . true God from true God . . . , of one
Being with the Father". So within this "he"—and indivisible
from him—there is contained another Self: the Father, with
whom he is of one Being, so that he can be said to be God
from God. That means: the first and true agent in this sentence, the subject, is—as we could hardly imagine to be other-

wise, in view of what we have just recalled—God, but God in three Persons, who yet are but one: the Father, the Son, and the Holy Spirit. But the dramatic feature of this sentence is that it does not assert some eternal truth about the being of God; rather, it expresses an action, which on closer inspection turns out to be in the passive voice, something that happens to him. It is to the action thus described, in which the three Divine Persons all play a part, that the "ex Maria virgine" refers; indeed, the dramatic aspect of the whole depends on it. For without Mary the entire process of God's stepping into history would fail of its object, would fail to achieve that very thing which is central in the Creed—that God is a God with us and not just a God in himself and for himself.

Thus, the woman who described herself as a lowly, that is, a nameless, woman (Lk 1:48),[1] stands beside the living God at the heart of the Creed, and it is inconceivable that she should not. She has an indisputable place in our belief in the living and acting God. The Word becomes flesh—the eternal foundation of the world's significance enters into it. He does not just observe it from without; he himself becomes an active agent within it. For this to be able to happen, the Virgin was needed, who made available her whole person, that is, her body, herself, that it might become the place of God's dwelling in the world. The Incarnation required acceptance. Only thus could Word and flesh become truly one. "He who created you without your aid did not wish to redeem you without your aid", was what Augustine said about it.[2] The

---

[1] Cf. on this point F. Mußner, *Maria, die Mutter Jesu im Neuen Testament* (St. Ottilien, 1993), pp. 45f.: "'ταπεινος' means of no account, small, poor, insignificant . . . 'henceforth', that will be quite different: Mary will no longer remain the unnnoticed, 'anonymous' girl; her name will, rather, become significant for all generations to come."

[2] Augustine, *Sermo* 169, cap. 11, no. 13 (PL 38:923); cf. Bonaventure, *Breviloquium*, pars 5, cap. 3.

"world" into which the Son came, the "flesh" that he took upon him, was not just somewhere or something or other—this world, this flesh was a person, an open heart. On the basis of the Psalms, the Letter to the Hebrews interpreted the process of incarnation as an actual dialogue within the Divinity: "A body have you prepared for me", says the Son to the Father (Heb 10:5). But this preparing of the body was achieved through Mary's also saying: "Sacrifices and offerings you have not desired, but a body have you prepared for me . . . . Behold, I have come to do your will" (Heb 10:5–7; Ps 40:6–8). The body was prepared for the Son, through Mary's putting herself entirely at the disposal of the Father's will and thus making her body available as the tabernacle of the Holy Spirit.

2. The Biblical Background to This Sentence

In order to comprehend the central sentence of the Creed in all its profundity, we have to go back behind the Creed to its source: Holy Scripture. When we look more closely at this point in the Creed, it is seen to be a synthesis of the three great biblical witnesses to the Incarnation of the Son: Matthew 1:18–25; Luke 1:26–38; John 1:13f. Without going into detailed exegesis of these texts, let us try to get some idea of the particular contribution each one makes to our understanding of the Incarnation of God.

2.1 *Matthew 1:18–25*

Matthew is writing his Gospel for a Jewish and Jewish Christian readership. So his concern is to demonstrate the continuity of the Old and New Covenants. The Old Testament points toward Jesus; in him its promises are fulfilled. The inner connection between expectation and fulfillment serves at the same time to demonstrate that it is really God who is at work and that Jesus is the Savior of the world sent by God. It is this viewpoint that determines, in the first place, the way Matthew sets the figure of Saint Joseph in the foreground in recounting the childhood stories, so as to show that Jesus is a son of David, the promised heir who will uphold the Davidic dynasty and will transform its kingdom into the kingship of God over all the world. The genealogy, in its character as a Davidic genealogy, leads down to Joseph. In the dream, the angel addresses Joseph as son of David (Mt 1:20). On this account it is Joseph who gives Jesus his name: "The acceptance of him as a son is completed by giving him his name."[3]

Precisely because Matthew wishes to show the connection between promise and fulfillment, the figure of the Virgin Mary makes her appearance beside that of Joseph. The promise God made through the prophet Isaiah to the doubting king Ahaz, who in the face of the oncoming enemy army did not wish to ask for a sign from God, still hung in the air, unapplied and incomprehensible. "The Lord himself will give you a sign. Behold, a virgin shall conceive and bear a son, and shall call his name Immanuel [God with us]" (Is 7:14). No one can say what this sign may have meant in the historical time of King Ahaz—whether it was indeed given or in what it consisted. The promise reached far beyond that hour of history. It hung above the history of Israel, moreover, like a star of hope, pointing to the future, pointing into the unknown. For Matthew, the veil has been drawn aside with the

[3] J. Gnilka, *Das Matthäusevangelium*, vol. 1 (Freiburg, 1986), p. 19.

birth of Jesus from the Virgin Mary: the sign has now been
given. The virgin, who by the power of the Holy Spirit
conceives as a virgin—she is the sign. And there is a new
name associated with this second line of promise, a name that
alone gives the name of Jesus its full significance and depth.
If the child mentioned in the promise of Isaiah is called
Emmanuel, then immediately the framework of the davidic
promise is expanded. The kingdom of this child stretches
beyond anything that the Davidic promise might lead us to
expect: his kingdom is the Kingdom of God himself; it shares
in the universality of God's rule, since in his person God
himself has stepped into the history of the world. It is of
course not until the last few verses of the Gospel that the
proclamation is again made of what is thus being shown in
the story of Jesus' conception and birth. In the course of his
earthly life Jesus knows that he must keep strictly to the house
of Israel, that he has not yet been sent to the nations of the
world. But after his death on the Cross the resurrected Jesus
says: "Make disciples of all the nations. . . . And behold, I am
with you always, to the close of the age" (Mt 28:19f.). Here
he is showing himself as the God-with-us whose new Kingdom comprises all the nations, because God is the same for
all. In the story of the conception of Jesus, Matthew makes a
corresponding alteration at one place in the Isaianic oracle.
He no longer says: She [the virgin] will give him the name
Emmanuel, but: They will call him Emmanuel, God with
us. In this word "they" appears a reference to the future
community of the faithful, the Church, who will call upon
Jesus by this name.[4] Everything in the narrative of Saint Matthew is oriented toward Christ, because everything is oriented toward God. That is how the Creed has quite rightly

[4] Ibid., p. 21.

understood it and has transmitted it to the Church. But because God is with us, then, the human agents who bear the
promise are of great importance: Joseph and Mary. Joseph
stands for God's faithfulness to his promises to Israel, but
Mary embodies the hope of mankind. Joseph is father according to the law, but Mary is mother with her own body:
it is on account of her that God has been able to become one
of us.

2.2 *Luke 1:26–38*

Let us now glance at the way Luke portrays the conception
and birth of Jesus—not in order to offer here any interpretation of that text, with its wealth of allusions, but simply
so as to understand the particular contribution it makes to the
statement in the Creed. I am restricting myself to the peri-
cope of the Annunciation of the birth of Jesus by the archan-
gel Gabriel (Lk 1:26–38). Luke lets the words of the angel
express the mystery of the Trinity and thus gives this event
the same theological center to which the whole of salvation
history is related in the Creed. The child who is being born
will be called Son of the Most High, Son of God; the Holy
Spirit, as the power of the Most High, will bring about this
conception in mysterious fashion; thus, the Son, the Father
(indirectly), and the Holy Spirit are all mentioned. For the
way that the Holy Spirit will come upon Mary, Luke uses
here the word "overshadow" (verse 35). He is thereby allud-
ing to the Old Testament story of the holy cloud that rested
over the Tent of Meeting to show when God was present.
Thus Mary is characterized as the new holy Tent, the living
ark of the Covenant. Her Yes becomes the place of meeting
that offers God a dwelling place in the world. God, who does
not live in stones, does live in this Yes that has been given

with body and soul; he who cannot be contained within the world can come to dwell in his entirety within one person. There are several traces in Luke of this theme of the new temple, of the true ark of the Covenant, especially, for instance, in the angel's greeting to Mary: Hail, full of grace! The Lord is with you (1:28). Nowadays it is hardly disputed that this saying of the angel, as Luke has transmitted it, takes up the oracle of promise in Zephaniah 3:14, which is addressed to the daughter of Zion and proclaims that God will dwell in her midst. Thus, this greeting presents Mary as the daughter of Zion personified and, at the same time, as the divine dwelling place, as the holy tent above which hangs the cloud of God's presence.[5] This idea was taken up by the Fathers and also influenced early Christian iconography. Saint Joseph is designated as high priest by his sprouting staff and as archetype of the Christian bishop. Mary, however, is the living Church. The Holy Spirit is coming down on her, and thus she becomes the new Temple. Joseph, the righteous man, is appointed steward of the mysteries of God—the head of the house and guardian of the sanctuary constituted by the bride and the Logos within her. Thus he becomes the image of the bishop, to whom the bride is entrusted; she is placed, not at his disposal, but in his safekeeping.[6] Everything here is ordered with respect to the trinitarian God, but for that very reason his presence with us in human history, in the mystery of Mary and the Church, is especially clear and comprehensible.

[5] Cf. S. M. Iglesias, *Los evangelios de la infancia*, vol. 2 (Madrid, 1986), pp. 149–60; J. Ratzinger, "Du bist voll der Gnade", in J. Ratzinger and P. Henrici, *Credo* (Cologne, 1992), pp. 103–16, especially pp. 105–9.

[6] What I say here is based on an unpublished study by A. Thiermeyer, *Josef als Idealbild des frühchristlichen Bischofs und Priesters* [Joseph as the ideal image of the early Christian bishop and priest] (Rome, 1989), which offers an interpretation of the iconography of the triumphal arch of the Church of Santa Maria Maggiore based on contemporary texts from the Church Fathers.

There is one other point in Luke's story of the Annunciation that seems to me important for the question we are considering. God asks man to consent. He does not simply dispose things as he wishes through his own power. In this creature, man, he has created a free being to stand over against him, and he now has need of the freedom of this creature, that his Kingdom may truly come to be, that Kingdom which is based, not upon external power, but upon freedom. In one of his sermons, Bernard of Clairvaux has depicted in dramatic fashion this waiting of God and the waiting of mankind:

> The angel awaits your answer, for it is time for him to return to the One who sent him. . . . O Lady, answer with the word that earth and hell and, yes, even heaven are waiting for. Just as the Lord and King yearned for your beauty, so equally now he longs for you to respond with your agreement. . . . Why are you hesitating? Why are you fearful? . . . Behold, the One for whom all peoples are longing stands without and knocks on the door. Ah, what if he were to pass on because you hesitated. . . . Stand up, hasten, open up! Stand up in faith, hasten in your devotion, open up by your assent![7]

Without the freely given assent of Mary, God cannot become man. Certainly, this Yes Mary says is wholly by grace. The dogma of the Immaculate Conception of Mary, whereby she was freed from original sin, has in fact just exactly this as its sole significance: that no human being can set in motion the process of salvation by his own powers alone, but that his Yes is wrapped around and supported within by that divine

[7] Bernard of Clairvaux, *In laudibus Virginis Matris*, homily 4, 8, in *Opera omnia*, edit. Cisterc. 4 (1966), pp. 53f.; in the Latin-German edition of the *Werke* of Saint Bernard, edited by G. Winkler, vol. 4 (Innsbruck, 1993), p. 112: "Quid tardas? Quid trepidas? . . . In hac sola re ne timeas, prudens Virgo, praesumptionem. . . . Aperi, Virgo beata, cor fidei, labia confessioni, viscera Creatori. Ecce desideratus cunctis gentibus foris pulsat ad ostium. O si, te morante, pertransierit. . . . Surge, curre, aperi!"

love which comes first and before all else and that already surrounds man before he is even born. "All is grace." Yet grace does not remove freedom; rather, it brings it into being. The entire mystery of redemption is present in this story and is summed up in the figure of the Virgin Mary: "Behold, I am the handmaid of the Lord; let it be to me according to your word" (Lk 1:38).

2.3 *The Prologue of John*

Let us turn to the prologue of the Gospel of John, the wording of which is taken as a basis for the Creed. Here, too, I would just like to pick out three salient points. "The Word was made flesh and pitched his tent among us" (1:14). The Word became flesh: we have become so accustomed to this expression that we are no longer struck by that enormous divine synthesis of apparently irreconcilably divided elements, into the understanding of which the Fathers found their way step by step. This is where the genuinely new element of Christianity was, and still is, to be found: that element which seemed to the Greek mind absurd and unthinkable. What is said here does not spring from some particular culture, Semitic, for instance, or Greek, as people nowadays repeatedly and thoughtlessly assert. It runs counter to every cultural model known to us. It was just as absurd for the Jews as it was, on quite different grounds, for the Greeks, or for the Indians, or, come to that, as it is for the modern mind, for whom this synthesis of the phenomenal and religious spheres appears quite unreal and who therefore renews the attack on it with all the self-consciousness of modern rationality. What is said here is "new" because it comes from God and could only be brought about by God. It is something entirely new and strange to any and every culture, throughout history, into which we can enter in faith, and only in faith, and which opens up for us entirely new horizons of thought and of life.

But John has another, quite different emphasis in mind here. The clause concerning the Logos that becomes *sarx*, flesh, points forward to chapter six of the Gospel, the whole of which unfolds the meaning of this half-verse.[8] In that passage Jesus declares to the Jews and to the world: The Bread that I give (that is, the Logos that is the true nourishment of man) is my flesh for the life of the world (6:51). This saying about Christ's flesh expresses at the same time his self-giving sacrifice, the mystery of the Cross and the mystery of the paschal sacrament that derives from it. The Word does not simply become flesh in some way or other, just to achieve a new status. The dynamic of sacrifice is comprehended in the Incarnation. Hidden within it again is the saying from the psalm: "A body have you prepared for me" (Heb 10:5; Ps 40). Thus, the entire Gospel is contained within this single statement; we are reminded of the saying of the Fathers that the Logos has contracted, has become small. This is true in two senses: the infinite Logos has become small, become a child. But also: the immeasurable Word, the entire fullness of Holy Scripture, has contracted itself within the compass of this one sentence, which gathers together the law and the prophets.[9] Being and history, cult and ethics are united and are present without abbreviation there in the christological center.

[8] Cf. R. Schnackenburg, *Das Johannesevangelium*, vol. 1 (Freiburg, 1965), p. 243.

[9] Cf. H. U. von Balthasar, "Das Wort verdichtet sich" [The Word becomes dense], *Internationale katholische Zeitschrift Communio* 6 (1977): 397–400. To those texts from Origen, Gregory Nazianzen, and Maximus the Confessor, to which von Balthasar refers, one might add, as a typically Western formulation of the same theme, Augustine, *Tractatus in Johannem* 17:7f. (CCL 36, pp. 174f.)

The second reference I want to make can be quite brief. John speaks of the dwelling of God as being the result and the purpose of the Incarnation. In this connection he uses the word for pitching a tent and thus once more refers back to the Tent of Meeting in the Old Testament, to the theology of the Temple, which finds fulfillment in the incarnate Logos. But in the Greek word for tent—*skene*—we hear overtones of the Hebrew word *shekhina*, that is to say, the term used in early Judaism to refer to the sacred cloud, which then became simply a name for God and proclaimed "the gracious presence of God at the prayer and the study of the law whenever Jews were gathered together".[10] Jesus is the true *shekhina*, through whom God is present among us whenever we are gathered together in his name.

Finally, we need just to glance at verse 13. To those who received him, he—the Logos—gave the power to become children of God: "to all who believed in his name", "who were born, not of blood nor of the will of the flesh nor of the will of man, but of God". Two different forms of this verse have been transmitted in the textual witnesses, and today we can no longer decide which is the original. Both appear almost equally early, and their witnesses have equal weight. That is to say, there is a singular version: "who was born not of blood, nor of the will of the flesh, nor of the will of man, but of God." And side by side with that is the plural version familiar to us: "who were born . . . of God".[11]

---

[10] Schnackenburg, *Johannesevangelium*, 1:245.

[11] In 1965 (*Johannesevangelium*, 1:241), Schnackenburg was still saying: "Although both readings are old, we would nonetheless have to regard the plural reading as the original one." He maintained the same position, against J. Galot, in his first additional appendix to this first volume, in the third edition, in 1972 (*Johannesevangelium*, 4:191); in the second additional appendix (to the fourth edition, in 1978), in view of what had been published by M. Vellanikkal, I. de la Potterie, and P. Hofrichter, he left the question open.

This double form of transmission is comprehensible, because in each case the verse refers to both agents. In that sense, we actually need always to read both versions together, because only between them do they present the whole meaning of the text. If we take the usual plural version as our starting point, this refers to those who are baptized, who have been granted the new divine birth from the Logos. But the mystery of the virgin birth of Jesus, which is the origin of this divine birth of ours, can so clearly be seen beyond it that only a prejudiced mind could deny this connection. Yet even if we take the singular form as being the original, the reference to "all who received him" remains quite obvious. It is becoming clear that Jesus' conception from God, his new birth, is for the purpose of including us, of bringing new birth to us.

Just as verse 14, which speaks of the Word becoming flesh, points forward to the eucharistic chapter of the Gospel, so here there is an unmistakable allusion to the conversation with Nicodemus in chapter 3. Christ says to Nicodemus that it is not enough to be born in the flesh in order to enter into the Kingdom of God. New birth from on high is needed, a rebirth from water and spirit (3:5). Christ, who was conceived by the Virgin through the power of the Holy Spirit, is the beginning of a new humanity, of a new way of living. To become a Christian means to be brought in to share in this new beginning. Becoming a Christian is more than turning to new ideas, to a new morality, to a new community. The transformation that happens here has all the drastic quality of a real birth, of a new creation. But in this sense the Virgin Mother is once more standing at the center of the redemption event. With her whole being, she stands surety for the new thing that God has brought about. Only if her story is true, and stands at the beginning, can what Paul says be true:

"Therefore, if any one is in Christ, he is a new creation" (2
Cor 5:17).

3. The Footprints of God

God is not tied down to stones, but he does tie himself down
to living people. The Yes of Mary opens for him the place
where he can pitch his tent. She herself becomes a tent for
him, and thus she is the beginning of the Holy Church,
which in her turn points forward to the New Jerusalem, in
which there is no temple any more, because God himself
dwells in her midst. The faith in Christ that we confess in the
Creed of the baptized people thus becomes a spiritualization
and a purification of everything that was ever said or hoped,
in the history of religions, about God's dwelling in the world.
Yet it is at the same time an embodiment of God's being with
men, which renders this concrete and particular, going far
beyond anything that might have been hoped for. "God is in
the flesh"—this indissoluble association of God with his creature, in particular, is what constitutes the heart of the Christian faith. Since this is so, it is understandable that from the
beginning Christians regarded as sacred those places at which
this event had taken place. They became an enduring guarantee of God's entering into the world. Thus Nazareth, Bethle-
hem, and Jerusalem became places at which one can, as it
were, see the footprints of the Redeemer, places where the
mystery of the Incarnation of God touches us directly.

As far as the story of the Annunciation is concerned, the
Protoevangelium of James, which, after all, goes back to the
second century and which, in spite of its many legendary
elements, may also have preserved genuine memories, has
assigned this event to two separate places. Mary

took the pitcher and went forth to draw water, and behold, a voice said: "Hail, thou that art highly favoured, the Lord is with thee, blessed art thou among women." And she looked around on the right and on the left to see whence this voice came. And trembling she went to her house and put down the pitcher and took the purple and sat down on her seat and drew out the thread. And behold, an angel of the Lord suddenly stood before her and said: "Do not fear, Mary, for you have found grace before the Almighty and shall conceive of his Word" (*Prot. James* 11:1).[12]

Corresponding to this dual tradition there are the two shrines, the Oriental shrine at the well and the Catholic basilica, which is built around the cave of the Annunciation. Both have a profound significance. Origen has drawn attention to the way that the theme of the well is determinative for the Old Testament patriarchal stories as a whole.[13] Wherever they went, they dug wells. Water is the basic element of life. Thus the well increasingly emerges as the image for life itself, right up to the well of Jacob, at which Jesus reveals himself as the wellspring of true life, the one for which the deepest thirst of mankind has been waiting. The well, the springing water, becomes a sign for the mystery of Christ, who offers us the water of life and from whose opened side flow blood and water. The well becomes a proclamation of Christ. But side

[12] The German text is found in E. Hennecke and W. Schneemelcher, *Neutestamentliche Apokryphen*, vol. 1: *Evangelien* (Tübingen, 1959), pp. 280–90, quotation no. 284. See the important introduction by O. Cullmann, pp. 277–79. [English trans. by R. M. Wilson: *New Testament Apocrypha*, vol. 1, *Gospels and Related Writings* (1963; reprinted by SCM Press, 1973). Cullmann's introduction is found on pp. 370–74, the text of *Prot. James* on pp. 374–88, and the quotation on p. 380.]

[13] See the marvelous passage in the *Homilies on Genesis* 13:1–4, GCS vol. 29, *Origenes Werke*, ed. Baehrens, 6:113–21; German translation by H. U. von Balthasar in *Origenes: Geist und Feuer*, 3d ed. (Einsiedeln, 1991), pp. 39–44. Cf. also J. Corbon, *Liturgie aus dem Urquell* (Einsiedeln, 1981), pp. 17f.

by side with this stands the house, the place of prayer and of recollection. "When you pray, go into your room" (Mt 6:6). The intensely personal event, the Annunciation of the Incarnation and the Virgin's response, demands a discreet domestic setting. The researches of B. Bagatti have revealed that, as early as the second century, someone's hand had scratched in Greek on the wall of the cave at Nazareth the words of the angel's greeting to Mary: Hail Mary.[14] Gianfranco Ravasi makes the beautifully appropriate remark: The evidence of this research underlines for us the fact "that the Christian message is not a collection of abstract propositions about God but is God's encounter with our world, with the reality of our homes and our lives".[15] That is exactly what is at issue here, at the Holy House of Loreto, and in the year of its great Jubilee:[16] We let ourselves be touched by the concrete character of God's action, so that with renewed gratitude and conviction we can say: He was born of the Virgin Mary and became man.

---

[14] G. Ravasi, *I Vangeli di Natale* [The birth and infancy gospels] (Società S. Paolo, 1992), pp. 45 and 54.

[15] Ibid., p. 54.

[16] This was written as an introductory address for the mariological congress held on the occasion of the seventh centenary of this sanctuary (March 1995).

God's Yes and His Love
Are Maintained Even in Death

The Origin of the Eucharist in the Paschal Mystery

Some years ago, Gonsalves Mainberger—who was at that time still a member of the Order of Preachers—shocked his audience in Zürich, and soon after that his readers right across Europe, with the assertion: "Christ died for nothing." Exactly what he meant by that remained to some extent obscure; he was probably trying to translate into a striking slogan what we can read in Bultmann's writings in the cautious phrasing of the scholar. Bultmann says: We do not know how Jesus met his death, how he endured it. We must leave open the possibility of his having failed.[1] To understand this, we must have in mind how Bultmann himself portrays Jesus. On the basis of the supposition that everywhere and always only normal and probable things can actually happen, that the miracle of something wholly other is historically impossible, he strips away from Jesus all that is unusual, extraordinary, or even divine.[2] What is left in the end is an

For the context of this selection, see note at List of Sources, page 155.

[1] R. Bultmann, *Das Verhältnis der urchristlichen Christusbotschaft zum historischen Jesus* (Heidelberg, 1960). For the contemporary discussion among exegetes, see: K. Kertelge, ed., *Der Tod Jesu: Deutungen im Neuen Testament* (Freiburg, 1976); and H. Schürmann, *Jesu ureigener Tod* (Freiburg, 1975).

[2] Cf. on this point the important essay of H. Schlier, which may mark a turning point in the treatment of this subject: "Zur Frage: Wer ist Jesus?", in J. Gnilka, ed., *Neues Testament und Kirche. Für R. Schnackenburg* (Freiburg, 1974), pp. 359–70.

average sort of rabbi, such as might have lived in any age.
Then it certainly does become incomprehensible for this rabbi
suddenly to end up on the Cross, since people do not crucify
the average professor. So it is not actually the real Jesus who
breaks down on the Cross, but this notional Jesus does come
to grief there. Seen from the viewpoint of the Cross, it
becomes clear that Jesus was the kind of person who transcends all normal standards and who cannot be explained in
normal terms. It would otherwise be incomprehensible for
groups hostile to one another, Jews and Romans, believers
and atheists, to join together to rid themselves of this remarkable prophet. He just did not fit into any of the ready-made
categories people use, and therefore they had to clear him out
of the way. There, again, it becomes clear that we cannot get
to know the real Jesus by trimming him to fit our normal
standards. Only the Jesus of the witnesses is the real Jesus.
There is no better way of learning about him than to listen to
the word of those who lived with him, who accompanied
him along the paths of this earthly life.

If we question these witnesses, then we see—and this is in
fact self-evident—that it was by no means a surprise to Jesus,
something quite unforeseen, when he ended up on the Cross.
He could hardly have been blind to the storm brewing up, to
the force of the contradiction, enmity, and rejection that was
gathering round him. It was of no less significance for his
walking on toward the Cross with his eyes open that he lived
from the heart of the faith of Israel, that he prayed the prayer
of his people with them: the Psalms, which were inspired by
the prophets and expressed the religion of Israel, are deeply
marked by the figure of the righteous man who suffers, who
for the sake of God can no longer find any place in this
world, who for the sake of his faith endures suffering. Jesus
appropriated this prayer, which we can see springing ever

new, with ever deeper tones, both in the Psalms and in the prophets, from the Servant of Second Isaiah right up to Job and to the three young men in the fiery furnace; he made it intimately his own, filled it out, offered his own self for its sake, and thereby finally gave the key that opened up this prayer.[3]

Thus, in his preaching all paths lead into the mystery of him who proves the truth of his love and his message in suffering. The words he spoke at the Last Supper then represent the final shaping of this. They offer nothing entirely unexpected, but rather what has already been shaped and adumbrated in all these paths, and yet they reveal anew what was signified throughout: the institution of the Eucharist is an anticipation of his death; it is the undergoing of a spiritual death. For Jesus shares himself out, he shares himself as the one who has been split up and torn apart into body and blood. Thus, the *eucharistic words* of Jesus are the answer to Bultmann's question about how Jesus underwent his death; in these words he undergoes a spiritual death, or, to put it more accurately, *in these words Jesus transforms death into the spiritual act of affirmation, into the act of self-sharing love;* into the act of adoration, which is offered to God, then from God is made available to men. Both are essentially interdependent: the words at the Last Supper without the death would be, so to speak, an issue of unsecured currency; and again, the death without these words would be a mere execution without any discernible point to it. Yet the two together constitute this new event, in which the senselessness of death is given

---

[3] There is much valuable material on this in H. J. Kraus, *Psalmen*, vols. 1 and 2 (Neukirchen, 1960) [English trans. by H. C. Oswald, *Psalms 1–59* and *Psalms 60–150*, (Fortress Press, 1988–1989)]; and in H. U. von Balthasar, *Herrlichkeit*, vol. 3, pt. 2, *Alter Bund* (Einsiedeln, 1967) [English trans., *The Glory of the Lord*, vol. 6, *Theology: The Old Covenant*, trans. Brian McNeil and Erasmo Leiva-Merikakis (San Francisco: Ignatius Press, 1991)].

meaning; in which what is irrational is transformed and made rational and articulate; in which the destruction of love, which is what death means in itself, becomes in fact the means of verifying and establishing it, of its enduring constancy. If, then, we want to know how Jesus himself intended his death to be understood, how he accepted it, what it means, then we must reflect on these words; and, contrariwise, we must regard them as being constantly guaranteed by the pledge of the blood that was his witness.

Before we look at them more closely, let us just cast a glance at the great drama that Saint John has unfolded in the thirteenth chapter of his Gospel—in the story of the *washing of the disciples' feet*. In this scene, the evangelist sums up, as it were, the whole of Jesus' message, his life, and his Passion. As if in a vision, we see what this whole really is.[4] In the washing of the disciples' feet is represented for us what Jesus does and what he is. He, who is Lord, comes down to us; he lays aside the garments of glory and becomes a slave, one who stands at the door and who does for us the slave's service of washing our feet. This is the meaning of his whole life and Passion: that he bends down to our dirty feet, to the dirt of humanity, and that in his greater love he washes us clean. The slave's service of washing the feet was performed in order to prepare a person suitably for sitting at table, to make him ready for company, so that all could sit down together for a meal. Jesus Christ prepares us, as it were, for God's presence and for each other's company, so that we can sit down together at table. We, who repeatedly find we cannot stand one another, who are quite unfit to be with God, are welcomed and accepted by him. He clothes himself, so to speak, in the garment of

---

[4] Cf. H. Schürmann, *Der Geist macht lebendig* [The Spirit brings life] (Freiburg, 1972), pp. 116–25, and similarly the commentaries on the Gospel of John by R. Bultmann and R. Schnackenburg.

our poverty, and in being taken up by him, we are able to be with God, we have gained access to God. We are washed through our willingness to yield to his love. The meaning of this love is that God accepts us without preconditions, even if we are unworthy of his love, incapable of relating to him, because he, Jesus Christ, transforms us and becomes a brother to us.

Certainly, John's account shows us that even where God sets no limits, man can sometimes do so. Two such instances appear here. The first becomes apparent in the figure of Judas: There is the No stemming from greed and lust, from vainglory, which refuses to accept God. This is the No given because we want to make the world for ourselves and are not ready to accept it as a gift from God. "Sooner remain in debt than pay with a coin that does not bear our own portrait—that is what our sovereignty demands", as Nietzsche once said.[5] The camel will not go through the eye of the needle; it sticks its proud hump up, so to speak, and is thus unable to get through the gate of merciful kindness. I think we all ought to ask ourselves, right now, whether we are not just like those people whose pride and vainglory will not let them be cleansed, let them accept the gift of Jesus Christ's healing love. Besides this refusal, which arises from the greed and the pride of man, there is, however, also the danger of piety, represented by Peter: the false humility that does not want anything so great as God bending down to us; the false humility in which pride is concealed, which dislikes forgiveness and would rather achieve its own purity; the false pride and the false modesty that will not accept God's mercy. But God does not wish for false modesty that refuses his kindness; rather, he desires that humility which allows itself to

[5] *Fröhliche Wissenschaft* [Joyful wisdom] 3:252; quoted from J. Pieper, *Über den Begriff der Sünde* (Munich, 1977), p. 120.

be cleansed and thus becomes pure. This is the manner in which he gives himself to us.

Let us now turn again to Jesus' words at the Last Supper, as they are recounted to us in the first three Gospels, and let us ask what we find there. We have in the first place these two immeasurably profound sayings, which stand for all time at the heart of the Church, at the heart of the eucharistic celebration, the sayings from which we draw our life, because these words are the presence of the living God, the presence of Jesus Christ in our midst, and thereby they tear the world free from its unbearable boredom, indifference, sadness, and evil. *"This is my Body, this is my Blood"*: these are expressions taken from the Israelite language of sacrifice, which designated the gifts offered in sacrifice to God in the Temple.[6] If Jesus makes use of these words, then he is designating *himself* as *the true and ultimate sacrifice*, in whom all these unsuccessful strivings of the Old Testament are fulfilled. What had always been intended and could never be achieved in the Old Testament sacrifices is incorporated in him. God does not desire the sacrifice of animals; everything belongs to him. And he does not desire human sacrifice, for he has created man for living. God desires something more: he desires love, which transforms man and through which he becomes capable of relating to God, giving himself up to God. Now, all those thousands of sacrifices that were always presented to God in the Temple at Jerusalem and all the sacrifices performed in the whole course of history, all this vain and eternal striving to bring ourselves up to God, can be seen as unnecessary and yet, at the same time, as being like windows that allow us, so

[6] J. Jeremias, *Die Abendmahlsworte Jesu* [The eucharistic words of Jesus], 3d. ed. (Göttingen, 1960); J. Betz, *Die Eucharistie in der Zeit der griechischen Väter*, vol. 2, pt. 1: *Die Realpräsenz des Leibes und Blutes Jesu im Abendmahl nach dem Neuen Testament* (Freiburg, 1961).

to speak, a glimpse of the real thing, like preliminary attempts at what has now been achieved. What they signified—giving to God, union with God—comes to pass in Jesus Christ, in him who gives God nothing but himself and, thereby, us in him.

But we now have to ask: How does that happen, and what does that mean, more precisely? Here we meet with a second factor. To each of the phrases under consideration, which derive from the Temple theology of Israel or, alternatively, from the Sinai covenant, Jesus adds a saying that is taken from the book of Isaiah: "This is my body, *which is given for you*; my blood, *which is shed for you and for many.*" This phrase is taken from the Songs of the *Suffering Servant*, which we find in Isaiah (chap. 53).[7] We need briefly to cast a glance over their background in order to grasp their content. With the Babylonian exile, Israel had lost its Temple. It could no longer worship God; it could no longer offer up its praises; it could no longer present the sacrifices of atonement; and it was bound to ask what should happen now, how its relationship with God could be kept alive, how order could be maintained in the world's affairs. For that was what the cult was about, in the final analysis: maintaining the correct relationship between God and man, since only thus can the axis around which reality turns be kept true. Through these questionings, which necessarily arose in this period of the absence of the cult, Israel came to a new experience. It could no longer celebrate the Temple worship; it could only suffer for the sake of its God. The great minds of Israel, the prophets, were enlightened by God so as to understand that this suffering of

[7] Cf. J. Scharbert, "Stellvertretendes Sühneleiden in den Ebed-Jahwe-Liedern und in altorientalischen Ritualtexten", *Biblische Zeitschrift*, 1958, pp. 190–213; idem, "Die Rettung der 'Vielen' durch die 'Wenigen' im Alten Testament", *Trierer theologische Zeitschrift* 68 (1959): 146–61.

Israel is the true sacrifice, the great new form of worship, with which it could come before the living God on behalf of mankind, on behalf of the whole world. But there is still one point at which this remains incomplete: Israel is the suffering servant of God, who accepts God in his suffering and stands before God on behalf of the world, and yet it is at the same time stained and guilty and selfish and lost. It cannot play the part of the servant of God properly and completely. Thus, these great songs, in a remarkable fashion, remain indeterminate; on the one hand, they speak of the fate of the suffering people and offer an interpretation of this; they help people to accept their suffering as a positive response to the God who loves and who judges. But at the same time they open up an expectation of the one in whom this will all be entirely true, the one who will truly be the undefiled witness to God in this world and who cannot yet be named. At the Last Supper, Jesus takes this saying into his own mouth: He is suffering for the many, and he shows, thereby, that in him this expectation is fulfilled: that this great act of worship on the part of mankind comes to pass in his suffering. He himself is, so to speak, the pure representative, the one who does not stand on his own behalf, but stands before God on behalf of all.

At this point I should like to include a question about which some people argue in extremely heated fashion: The German translation no longer says, "for many", but "for all", and this takes into account that in the Latin Missal and in the Greek New Testament, that is to say, in the original text that is being translated, we find "for many". This disparity has given rise to some disquiet; the question is raised as to whether the text of the Bible is not being misrepresented, whether perhaps an element of untruth has been brought into the most sacred place in our worship. In this connection, I would like to make three points.

1. In the New Testament as a whole, and in the whole of the tradition of the Church, it has always been clear that God desires that everyone should be saved and that Jesus died, not just for a part of mankind, but for everyone; that God himself—as we were just saying—does not draw the line anywhere. He does not make any distinction between people he dislikes, people he does not want to have saved, and others whom he prefers; he loves everyone because he has created everyone. That is why the Lord died for all. That is what we find in Saint Paul's Letter to the Romans: God "did not spare his own Son but gave him up for us all" (8:32); and in the fifth chapter of the Second Letter to the Corinthians: "One has died for all" (2 Cor 5:14). The first Letter to Timothy speaks of "Christ Jesus, who gave himself as a ransom for all" (1 Tim 2:6). This sentence is particularly important in that we can see, by the context and by the way it is formulated, that a eucharistic text is being quoted here. Thus we know that at that time, in a certain part of the Church, the formula that speaks of a sacrifice "for all" was being used in the Eucharist. The insight that was thus preserved has never been lost from the tradition of the Church. On Maundy Thursday, in the old missal, the account of the Last Supper was introduced with the words: "On the evening before he died, for the salvation of all he . . . ." It was on the basis of this knowledge that in the seventeenth century there was an explicit condemnation of a Jansenist proposition that asserted that Christ did not die for everyone.[8] This limitation of salvation was thus explicitly rejected as an erroneous teaching that contradicted the faith of the whole Church. The teaching of the Church says exactly the opposite: Christ died for all.

We cannot start to set limits on God's behalf; the very heart

---

[8] Denzinger-Hünermann, no. 2005.

of the faith has been lost to anyone who supposes that it is only worthwhile, if it is, so to say, made worthwhile by the damnation of others. Such a way of thinking, which finds the punishment of other people necessary, springs from not having inwardly accepted the faith; from loving only oneself and not God the Creator, to whom his creatures belong. That way of thinking would be like the attitude of those people who could not bear the workers who came last being paid a denarius like the rest; like the attitude of people who feel properly rewarded only if others have received less. This would be the attitude of the son who stayed at home, who could not bear the reconciling kindness of his father. It would be a hardening of our hearts, in which it would become clear that we were only looking out for ourselves and not looking for God; in which it would be clear that we did not love our faith, but merely bore it like a burden. We must finally come to the point where we no longer believe it to be better to live without faith, standing around in the marketplace, so to speak, unemployed, along with the workers who were only taken on at the eleventh hour; we must be freed from the delusion that spiritual unemployment is better than living with the Word of God. We have to learn once more so to live our faith, so to assent to it, that we can discover in it that joy which we do not simply carry round with us because others are at a disadvantage, but with which we are filled, for which we are thankful, and which we would like to share with others. This, then, is the first point: It is a basic element of the biblical message that the Lord died for all—being jealous of salvation is not Christian.[9]

2. A second point to add to this is that God never, in any case, forces anyone to be saved. God accepts man's freedom.

---

[9] I have fully developed this idea in my little book *Vom Sinn des Christseins* (Munich, 1965), pp. 39ff.

He is no magician, who will in the end wipe out everything that has happened and wheel out his happy ending. He is a true father; a creator who assents to freedom, even when it is used to reject him. That is why God's all-embracing desire to save people does not involve the actual salvation of all men. He allows us the power to refuse. God loves us; we need only to summon up the humility to allow ourselves to be loved. But we do have to ask ourselves, again and again, whether we are not possessed of the pride of wanting to do it for ourselves; whether we do not rob man, as a creature, along with the Creator-God, of all his dignity and stature by removing all element of seriousness from the life of man and degrading God to a kind of magician or grandfather, who is unmoved by anything. Even on account of the unconditional greatness of God's love—indeed, because of that very quality—the freedom to refuse, and thus the possibility of perdition, is not removed.

3. What, then, should we make of the new translation? Both formulations, "for all" and "for many", are found in Scripture and in tradition. Each expresses one aspect of the matter: on one hand, the all-embracing salvation inherent in the death of Christ, which he suffered for all men; on the other hand, the freedom to refuse, as setting a limit to salvation. Neither of the two formulae can express the whole of this; each needs correct interpretation, which sets it in the context of the Christian gospel as a whole. I leave open the question of whether it was sensible to choose the translation "for all" here and, thus, to confuse translation with interpretation, at a point at which the process of interpretation remains in any case indispensable.[10] There can be no question

---

[10] The fact that in Hebrew the expression "many" would mean the same thing as "all" is not relevant to the question under consideration inasmuch as it is a question of translating, not a Hebrew text here, but a Latin text (from the

of misrepresentation here, since whichever of the formulations is allowed to stand, we must in any case listen to the whole of the gospel message: that the Lord truly loves everyone and that he died for all. And the other aspect: that he does not, by some magic trick, set aside our freedom but allows us to choose to enter into his great mercy.

Now let us turn back to look at yet a third saying in the Last Supper accounts: "This is the *new covenant* in my blood." We saw just now how Jesus, in accepting his death, gathers together and condenses in his person the whole of the Old Testament; first the theology of sacrifice, that is, everything that went on in the Temple and everything to do with the Temple, then the theology of the Exile, of the Suffering Servant. Now a third element is added, a passage from Jeremiah (31:31) in which the prophet predicts the New Covenant, which will no longer be limited to physical descendants of Abraham, no longer to the strict keeping of the law, but will spring from out of the new love of God that gives us a new heart. This is what Jesus takes up here. In his suffering and death this long-awaited hope becomes reality; his death seals the Covenant. It signifies something like a blood brotherhood between God and man. That was the idea underlying the way the Covenant had been depicted on Sinai. There, Moses had set up the altar to represent God and, over against it, twelve stones to represent the twelve tribes of Israel and had sprinkled them with blood, so as to associate God and man in the one communion of this sacrifice. What was there only a hesitant attempt is here achieved. He who is the Son of God, he who is man, gives himself to the Father in dying and thus shows

---

Roman Liturgy), which is directly related to a Greek text (the New Testament). The institution narratives in the New Testament are by no means simply a translation (still less, a mistaken translation) of Isaiah; rather, they constitute an independent source.

himself to be the one who *brings us all into the Father*. He now institutes true blood brotherhood, *a communion of God and man*; he opens the door that we could not open for ourselves. We can do no more than give a little tentative thought to God, and it is not in our power to know whether or not he responds. This remains the tragic element, the shadow hovering over so many religions, that they are simply a cry to which the response remains uncertain. Only God himself can hear the cry. Jesus Christ, both Son of God and man, who carries on his love right through death, who transforms death into an act of love and truth, he is the response; the Covenant is founded in him.

Thus we see how the Eucharist had its origin, what its true source is. The words of institution alone are not sufficient; the death alone is not sufficient; and even both together are still insufficient but have to be complemented by the Resurrection, in which God accepts this death and makes it the door into a new life. From out of this whole matrix—that he transforms his death, that irrational event, into an affirmation, into an act of love and of adoration—emerges his acceptance by God and the possibility of his being able to share himself in this way. On the Cross, Christ saw love through to the end. For all the differences there may be between the accounts in the various Gospels, there is one point in common: Jesus died praying, and in the abyss of death he upheld the First Commandment and held on to the presence of God.[11] Out of such a death springs this sacrament, the Eucharist.

We finally have to return to the question with which we

---

[11] This reflection was adumbrated by E. Käsemann in 1967, in an address at the Congress of the German Evangelical Church (published under the title: "Die Gegenwart des Gekreuzigten" [The presence of the Crucified], in E. Käsemann, *Kirchliche Konflikte*, vol. 1 [Göttingen, 1982], pp. 76–91, especially 77, 80f.).

started. Did Jesus fail? Well, he certainly was not successful in
the same sense as Caesar or Alexander the Great. From the
worldly point of view, he did fail in the first instance: he died
almost abandoned; he was condemned on account of his
preaching. The response to his message was not the great Yes
of his people, but the Cross. From such an end as that, we
should conclude that Success is definitely not one of the
names of God and that it is not Christian to have an eye to
outward success or numbers. God's paths are other than that:
his success comes about through the Cross and is always
found under that sign. The true witnesses to his authenticity,
down through the centuries, are those who have accepted
this sign as their emblem. When, today, we look at past
history, then we have to say that it is not the Church of the
successful people that we find impressive; the Church of
those popes who were universal monarchs; the Church of
those leaders who knew how to get on well with the world.
Rather, what strengthens our faith, what remains constant,
what gives us hope, is the Church of the suffering. She stands,
to the present day, as a sign that God exists and that man is not
just a cesspit, but that he can be saved. This is true of the
martyrs of the first three centuries, and then right up to
Maximilian Kolbe and the many unnamed witnesses who
gave their lives for the Lord under the dictatorships of our
own day; whether they had to die for their faith or whether
they had to let themselves be trampled on, day after day and
year after year, for his sake. The Church of the suffering gives
credibility to Christ: she is God's success in the world; the
sign that gives us hope and courage; the sign from which still
flows the power of life, which reaches beyond mere thoughts
of success and which thereby purifies men and opens up for
God a door into this world. So let us be ready to hear the call
of Jesus Christ, who achieved the great success of God on the

Cross; he who, as the grain of wheat that died, has become fruitful down through all the centuries; the Tree of Life, in whom even today men may put their hope.

The Wellspring of Life
from the Side of the Lord,
Opened in Loving Sacrifice

The Eucharist: Heart of the Church

John the evangelist has set his account of the Passion of Jesus Christ between two marvelous pictures, providing a kind of framework in which, in each case, he portrays the whole meaning of Jesus' life and suffering, so that he can then expound the origin of the Christian life, the origin and meaning of the sacraments. At the beginning of the Passion story stands the account of washing the disciples' feet; at the end, the solemn and moving account of the *opening of Jesus' side* (Jn 19:30–37). In constructing his narrative thus, John takes great care to establish which day it was that Jesus died.[1] It is clear in his Gospel that Jesus died at exactly the time when the paschal lambs were being sacrificed in the Temple for the feast of Passover. Thus, through the exact time of his death it becomes clear that he is the true Paschal Lamb, that the business with the lambs is finished, because the Lamb is come. For the side of Jesus, when it is pierced, John has chosen exactly the same word as is used in the creation story to tell of the creation

[1] We do not intend to reopen here the dispute about the historical accuracy of the synoptic or the Johannine chronology of the Passion; cf. on this point R. Pesch, *Das Markusevangelium*, vol. 2 (Freiburg, 1977), pp. 323–28.

of Eve, where we normally translate it as Adam's "rib".[2] In this fashion John makes it clear that Jesus is the New Adam, who goes down into the darkness of death's sleep and opens within it the beginning of a new humanity. From his side, that side which has been opened up in loving sacrifice, comes a spring of water that brings to fruition the whole of history. From the ultimate self-sacrifice of Jesus spring forth blood and water, Eucharist and baptism, as the source of a new community.

The Lord's opened side is the source from which spring forth both the Church and the sacraments that build up the Church. Thus what we were trying to comprehend in our first meditation is once more portrayed in this picture offered to us by the evangelist. The Last Supper alone is not sufficient for the institution of the Eucharist. For the words that Jesus spoke then are an anticipation of his death, a transformation of his death into an event of love, a transformation of what is meaningless into something that is significant, significant for us. But that also means that these words carry weight and have creative power for all time only in that they did not remain mere words but were given content by his actual death. And then again, this death would remain empty of meaning, his words would remain mere empty claims and unredeemed promises, were it not shown to be true that his love is stronger than death, that meaning is stronger than meaninglessness. The death would remain empty of meaning, and would also render the words meaningless, if the Resurrection had not come about, whereby it is made clear that these words were spoken with divine authority, that his love is indeed strong enough to reach out beyond death. Thus the three belong

[2] Cf. on this point H. Rahner, *Symbole der Kirche: Ekklesiologie der Väter* (Salzburg, 1964), pp. 177–205; and on the Jewish background, A. Tossato, *Il matrimonio nel Giudaismo Antico e nel Nuovo Testamento* (Rome, 1976), pp. 49–80.

together: the word, the death, and the Resurrection. And
this trinity of word, death, and Resurrection, which gives
us an inkling of the mystery of the triune God himself, this is
what Christian tradition calls the "Paschal Mystery", the
mystery of Easter. Only the three together make up a whole,
only these three together constitute a veritable reality, and
this single mystery of Easter is the source and origin of the
Eucharist.

But that means that the Eucharist is far more than just a
meal; it has cost a death to provide it, and the majesty of
death is present in it. Whenever we hold it, we should be
filled with reverence in the face of this mystery, with awe in
the face of this mysterious death that becomes a present
reality in our midst. Certainly, the overcoming of this death
in the Resurrection is present at the same time, and we can
therefore celebrate this death as the feast of life, as the transformation of the world. In all ages, and among all peoples,
the ultimate aim of men in their festivals has been to open
the door of death. For as long as it does not touch on this
question, a festival remains superficial, mere entertainment
to anaesthetize oneself. Death is the ultimate question, and
wherever it is bracketed out there can be no real answer. Only
when this question is answered can men truly celebrate and
be free. The Christian feast, the Eucharist, plumbs the very
depths of death. It is not just a matter of pious discourse
and entertainment, of some kind of religious beautification,
spreading a pious gloss on the world; it plumbs the very
depths of existence, which it calls death, and strikes out an
upward path to life, the life that overcomes death. And in this
way the meaning of what we are trying to reflect on, in this
meditation, becomes clear, what the tradition sums up in
this sentence: *The Eucharist is a sacrifice, the presentation of Jesus
Christ's sacrifice on the Cross.*

Whenever we hear these words, inhibitions arise within us, and in all ages it has always been so. The question arises: When we talk about sacrifice, do we not do so on the basis of an unworthy picture of God, or at least a naïve one? Does this not assume that we men should and could give something to God? Does this not show that we think of ourselves as equal partners with God, so to speak, who could barter one thing for another with him: we give him something so that he will give us something? Is this not to misapprehend the greatness of God, who has no need of our gifts, because he himself is the giver of all gifts? But, on the other hand, the question certainly does remain: Are we not all of us in debt to God, indeed, not merely debtors to him but offenders against him, since we are no longer simply in the position of owing him our life and our existence but have now become guilty of offenses against him? We cannot give him anything, and in spite of that we cannot even simply assume that he will regard our guilt as being of no weight, that he will not take it seriously, that he will look on man as just a game, a toy.

It is to this very question that the Eucharist offers us an answer.

First of all, it says this to us: *God himself gives to us, that we may give in turn.* The initiative in the sacrifice of Jesus Christ comes from God. In the first place it is he himself who comes down to us: "God so loved the world that he gave his only-begotten Son" (Jn 3:16). Christ is not in the first instance a gift *we* men bring to an angry God; rather, the fact that he is there at all, living, suffering, loving, is the work of God's love. He is the condescension of merciful love, who bows down to us; for us the Lord becomes a slave, as we saw in the previous meditation. It is in this sense that, in the Second Letter to the Corinthians, we find the words in which grace calls out to us: "Be reconciled to God" (2 Cor 5:20). Although *we* started the quarrel, although it is not God who owes us anything, but we him, he comes to meet us, and in Christ he begs, as it were, for reconciliation. He brings to be in reality what the Lord is talking about in the story of the gifts in the Temple, where he says: "If you are offering your gift at the altar, and there remember that your brother has something against you, leave your gift there before the altar and go; first be reconciled to your brother, and then come and offer your gift" (Mt 5:23f.). God, in Christ, has trodden this path before us; he has set out to meet us, his unreconciled children—he has left the temple of his glory and has gone out to reconcile us.

Yet we can already see the same thing if we look back to the beginning of the history of faith. Abraham, in the end, does not sacrifice anything he has prepared himself but offers the ram (the lamb) that has been offered to him by God. Thus, through this original sacrifice of Abraham a perspective opens up down the millennia; this lamb in the brambles that God gives him, so that he may offer it, is the first herald of that Lamb, Jesus Christ, who carries the crown of thorns of our guilt, who has come into the thorn bush of world history in order to give us something that we may give. Anyone who correctly comprehends the story of Abraham cannot come to the same conclusion as Tilman Moser in his strange and dreadful book *Poisoned by God*; Moser reads here the evidence for a God who is as dreadful as poison, making our whole life bitter.[3] Even when Abraham was still on his way, and as yet knew nothing of the mystery of the ram, he was able to say to Isaac, with trust in his heart: *Deus providebit*—God will take care of us. Because he knew this

---

[3] Cf., on the subject of T. Moser, the lovely contribution by O. H. Steck, "Ist Gott grausam?" [Is God cruel?] in W. Böhme, ed., *Ist Gott grausam? Eine Stellungnahme zu T. Mosers "Gottesvergiftung"* [Is God Cruel? Reactions to T. Moser's "Poisoned by God"] (Stuttgart, 1977), pp. 75–95.

God, therefore, even in the dark night of his incomprehension he knew that he is a loving God; therefore, even then, when he found he could understand nothing, he could put his trust in him and could know that the very one who seemed to be oppressing him truly loved him even then. Only in thus going onward, so that his heart was opened up, so that he entered the abyss of trust and, in the dark night of the uncomprehended God, dared keep company with him, did he thereby become capable of accepting the ram, of understanding the God who gives to us that we may give. This Abraham, in any case, has something to say to all of us. If we are only looking on from outside, if we only let God's action wash over us from without and only insofar as it is directed toward us, then we will soon come to see God as a tyrant who plays about with the world. But the more we keep him company, the more we trust in him in the dark night of the uncomprehended God, the more we will become aware that that very God who seems to be tormenting us is the one who truly loves us, the one we can trust without reserve. The deeper we go down into the dark night of the uncomprehended God and trust in him, the more we will discover him and will find the love and the freedom that will carry us through any and every night. God gives that we may give. This is the essence of the Eucharistic Sacrifice, of the sacrifice of Jesus Christ; from the earliest times, the Roman Canon has expressed it thus: "De tuis donis ac datis offerimus tibi"— from your gifts and offerings we offer you.

Even the second element—*we* offer—is absolutely true, not a mere fiction. So we must now ask: How can this come about—that, on the one hand, since we have nothing to give, God gives to us and that, on the other hand, we are not thereby reduced to mere passive objects of his action, who can only stand there in shame, but are on the contrary genuinely permitted to give him something? In order to understand that, we have to turn back again to the history of the people of Israel, whose faithful members engaged in a profound and passionate debate about what really constitutes a sacrifice and how it can be performed in a manner appropriate to God and to man. Out of this debate an insight gradually emerged, developed and consolidated in the religion of the prophets and of the psalmists, which might be expressed roughly in these words: A contrite spirit is the true sacrifice to offer you. May our prayers ascend to you like the smoke of incense. May our prayers to you carry more weight than the sacrifice of thousands of fat rams.

Israel was beginning to grasp that the sacrifice pleasing to God is a man pleasing to God and that prayer, the grateful praise of God, is thus the true sacrifice in which we give ourselves back to him, thereby renewing ourselves and the world. The heart of Israel's worship had always been what we express in the Latin word *memoriale*: *remembrance*. Whenever the Passover is celebrated, before the lamb is eaten, the head of the household recites the Passover Haggadah, that is to say, an account praising the great works God has done for Israel. The head of the house gives praise for the history God has made with his people, so that the next generation may hear it. But he does not recount this like mere past history; rather, he gives praise for the presence of God who supports us and who leads us, whose activity is thus present for us and in us. In the period in which Jesus lived, there was a growing consciousness of the Passover Haggadah as being at the real heart of Israel's worship, as being the true offering to God. The religion of Israel was at one here with the new religious outlook of the pagan world, in which the idea was emerging that the true sacrifice was the word or, rather, the man who in thanksgiving gave a spiritual dimension both to things and to himself, purified them, and thereby rendered them fit for God.

Now, it was into the texture of the Passover Haggadah, this thanksgiving prayer, that Jesus wove his sayings at the Last Supper, and it thereby acquired, over and above the shape it had developed in Israel, a new heart and center. It had hitherto remained merely verbal, in danger of turning into a mere form of words; it remained a verbal assertion in the midst of a history in which the victory of God is far from obvious, despite all his great works. Jesus Christ now gave to this prayer a heart that opens the locked door; this heart is his love, in which God is victorious and conquers death. The Canon of the Roman Mass developed directly from these Jewish prayers of thanksgiving; it is the direct descendant and continuation of this prayer of Jesus at the Last Supper and is thereby the heart of the Eucharist. It is the genuine vehicle of the sacrifice, since thereby Jesus Christ transformed his death into verbal form—into a prayer—and, in so doing, changed the world.[4] As a result, this death is able to be present for us, because it continues to live in the prayer, and the prayer runs right down through the centuries. A further consequence is that we can share in this death, because we can participate in this transforming prayer, can join in praying it. This, then, is the new sacrifice he has given us, in which he includes us all: Because he turned death into a proclamation of thanksgiving and love, he is now able to be present down through all ages as the wellspring of life, and we can enter into him by praying

---

[4] I have given a more complete account of the relations between these various elements in the article "Gestalt und Gehalt der eucharistischen Feier" [Form and content in the eucharistic celebration], which I contributed to the *Internationale katholische Zeitschrift Communio* 6 (1977): 385–96; reprinted, with two appendices, in J. Ratzinger, *Das Fest des Glaubens: Versuche zur Theologie des Gottesdienstes*, 3d ed. (Einsiedeln, 1993), pp. 31–54 [English trans., *The Feast of Faith*, trans. Graham Harrison (San Francisco: Ignatius Press, 1986), pp. 33–60].

with him. He gathers up, so to speak, the pitiful fragments of our suffering, our loving, our hoping, and our waiting into this prayer, into a great flood in which it shares in his life, so that thereby we truly share in the sacrifice.

Christ does not stand facing us alone. It was alone that he died, as the grain of wheat, but he does not arise alone, but as a whole ear of corn, taking with him the communion of the saints. Since the Resurrection, Christ no longer stands alone but is—as the Church Fathers say—always *caput et corpus*: head and body, open to us all. Thus he makes his word come true: "I, when I am lifted up from the earth, will draw all men to myself" (Jn 12:32). That is why we do not need to harbor the fear that motivated Luther to protest against the Catholic idea of the Mass as sacrifice, that thereby the glory of Christ might be diminished, or that the "sacrifice of the Mass" is founded on the idea that Christ's sacrifice was not enough and that we ought to, or could, add something to it. Such mistaken ideas may well have been current, but they have nothing to do with the real meaning of the concept of the sacrificial character of the Mass. The magnitude of Christ's achievement consists precisely in his not remaining someone else, over and against us, who might thus relegate us once more to a merely passive rôle; he does not merely bear with us; rather, he bears us up; he identifies himself with us to such an extent that our sins belong to him and his being to us: *he truly accepts us and takes us up, so that we ourselves become active with his support and alongside him, so that we ourselves cooperate and join in the sacrifice with him, participating in the mystery ourselves.* Thus our own life and suffering, our own hoping and loving, can also become fruitful, in the new heart he has given us.

Let us summarize what we have said so far. As a continuation of the Passover Haggadah, the Canon, as *eucharistia* (that

is, as the transformation of existence into thanksgiving), is the
true heart of the Mass. The Liturgy itself calls it *rationabile*
obsequium, an offering in verbal form. It presupposes in the
first place the spiritual struggle of the prophets, of the suffering men of righteousness in Israel, but equally the mature
religion of the Hellenistic world, which was increasingly close
to Judaism. But above all it shows an awareness that human
words can become true worship and sacrifice only if they are
given substance by the life and suffering of him who is himself the Word. The transforming of death into love, which is
achieved in his word of almighty power, thereby combines
human words with the Word of eternal love, which is what
the Son is, as he ceaselessly gives himself up in love to the
Father. That is why this word can do what human love merely
longs to do: open the door, in death, to resurrection. Thus
the Canon, the "true sacrifice", is the word of the Word; in it
speaks the one who, as Word, is life. By putting these words
into our mouths, letting us pronounce them with him, he
permits us and enables us to make the offering with him:
his words become our words, his worship our worship, his
sacrifice our sacrifice.

Following this farther, we now have to look at the structure of the Canon. In doing so we should note that the new
Eucharistic Prayers share the same structure as the traditional
Roman Canon; so that our reflections in respect of this one
instance are relevant in essentials to the others. So, when we
look at the so-called Roman Canon, we notice first of all
something quite remarkable: It does not talk only about God
and about Christ, his death and his Resurrection. It mentions
people by name: Sixtus, Clement, Cyprian; it allows us to
insert names, the names of people we have loved and who
have gone before us into the other world; the names of
people whom we would like to thank or whose burden we

would like to be able to share. Indeed, the Canon goes beyond this to speak of the whole creation, for when it says at
the close: "Through him you bless all these good gifts", then
it is envisaging everything we have received from God's good
hands; every one of our meals is, as it were, offered up in this
new feast that is Christ's gift to us and bears within it something of the new feast's thanksgiving to God the Creator. We
ought—I would add—to renew our awareness of this fact
that all our meals are alive with the goodness of God the
Creator, and all thereby point toward this greatest feast of all,
in which we receive no longer just earthly things, but the
incarnate act of God's mercy. We should resolve to make our
meals once more holy times, to open and to close them with
prayer. Doing this will introduce a new atmosphere into our
homes; wherever we pray together, where we receive God's
gifts with thankfulness, a new heart comes into being, which
also changes us ourselves.

We were saying that people are mentioned in the Canon;
there is a very simple reason for this. There is only *one* Christ.
Wherever the Eucharist is celebrated, he is wholly and fully
present. Because of that, even in the most humble village
church, when the Eucharist is celebrated, the whole mystery
of the Church, her living heart, the Lord, is present. But this
Christ, fully present, is yet at the same time one. That is why
we can only receive him together with everyone else. He is
the same, here or in Rome, in America or in Australia or
in Africa. Because he is one, we can only receive him in
unity. If ever we were opposed to unity, we would be unable
to meet with him. For that reason, every celebration of the
Eucharist has the structure we find in the *Communicantes*, that
of communion not only with the Lord but also with creation
and with men of all places and all times. This, too, is something we ought to take to heart anew, that we cannot have

communion with the Lord if we are not in communion with each other; that when we go to meet him in the Mass, we necessarily go to meet each other, to be at one with each other. Therefore the mentioning of the bishop and the pope by name, in the celebration of the Eucharist, is not merely an external matter, but an inner necessity of that celebration. For *the celebration of the Eucharist* is not just *a meeting of heaven and earth*; rather, it is also *a meeting of the Church then and now* and *a meeting of the Church here and there*; it assumes that we visibly enter into a visible unity, one that can be described. The names of the bishop and the pope stand for the fact that we are truly celebrating the *one* Eucharist of Jesus Christ, which we can receive only in the *one* Church.

Thus a final point becomes evident: at the heart of the Canon is the narrative of the evening before Jesus' Passion. When this is spoken, then the priest is not recounting the story of something that is past, just recalling what happened then, but something is taking place in the present. "This *is* my Body" is what is said now, today. But these words are the words of Jesus Christ. No man can pronounce them for himself. No one can, for his own part, declare his body to be the Body of Christ, declare this bread to be his Body, speaking in the first person, the "I" of Jesus Christ. This saying in the first person—"*my* Body"—only he himself can say. If anyone were to dare to say, on his own behalf, that he saw himself as the self of Christ, this would surely be blasphemy. No one can endow himself with such authority; no one else can give it to him; no congregation or community can give it to him. It can only be the gift of the Church as a whole, the one whole Church, to whom the Lord has communicated himself. *For this reason the Mass needs the person who does not speak in his own name, who does not come on his own authority, but who represents the whole Church, the Church of all places and all*

ages, which has passed on to him what was communicated to her.
The fact that the celebration of the Eucharist is tied to ordination as a priest is not, as we sometimes hear, something
that the Church has invented, by means of which she arro-
gates to herself all kinds of privileges and restricts the activity
of the Spirit. It follows from the essential significance of these
words, which no one has the right to pronounce on his own
behalf; it follows that these words can be pronounced only in
the sacrament of the Church as a whole, with the authority
that she alone, in her unity and her fullness, possesses. Being
entrusted with the mission that the whole Church in her
unity has herself received is what we call ordination to the
priesthood. On the basis of all this we ought to try to discover
a new reverence for the eucharistic mystery. Something is
happening there that is greater than anything we can do. The
magnitude of what is happening is not dependent on the way
we perform it, but all our efforts to perform it aright can
always be only at the service of the great act that precedes our
own and that we cannot achieve for ourselves. We should
learn anew that the Eucharist is never merely what a congregation does, but that we receive from the Lord what he
has granted to the entirety of the Church. I am always moved
by those stories of what happened in concentration camps
or Russian prison camps, where people had to do without
the Eucharist for a period of weeks or months and yet did
not turn to the arbitrary action of celebrating it themselves;
rather, they made a eucharistic celebration of their longing,
waiting with yearning upon the Lord, who alone can give of
himself. In such a Eucharist of longing and yearning they
were made ready for his gift in a new way, and they received
it as something new, when somewhere or other a priest found
a bit of bread and some wine.

On this basis, we should likewise accept the question of

intercommunion with appropriate humility and patience. It is not for us to act as if there were unity where this is not the case. The Eucharist is never the means we can use to any end; it is the gift of the Lord, the heart of the Church herself, and not within our control. It is not a matter of personal friendship here, of the strength of subjective faith, which in any case we have no means of measuring, but of standing within the unity of the one Church and of our humbly waiting for God to grant this unity himself. Instead of conducting experiments in this area and robbing the mystery of its greatness and degrading it to an instrument in our hands, we too should learn to celebrate a Eucharist of longing and yearning and in shared prayer and shared hope to walk together with the Lord toward new ways of finding unity.

Saint John's account of the Lord's death closes with the words: "They shall look on him whom they have pierced" (Jn 19:37 = Zech 12:10). He begins his Revelation with these words, which in that place constitute the opening of the Day of Judgment, that day on which the one who was pierced will rise over the world as its judgment and its life. But he commands us to look upon him now, so that the judgment may be turned to salvation. "They shall look on him whom they have pierced." This might be a description of the inner direction of our Christian life, our learning ever more truly to look upon him, to keep the eyes of our heart turned upon him, to see him, and thereby to grow more humble; to recognize our sins, to recognize how we have struck him, how we have wounded our brethren and thereby wounded him; to look upon him and, at the same time, to take hope, because he whom we have wounded is he who loves us; to look upon him and to receive the way of life. Lord, grant to us to look upon you and, in so doing, to find true life!

Banquet of the Reconciled
—Feast of the Resurrection

The Proper Celebration of the Holy Eucharist

When you assemble as a church, I hear that there are
divisions among you; and I partly believe it, for there must
be factions among you in order that those who are genuine
among you may be recognized. When you meet together,
it is not the Lord's supper that you eat. For in eating, each
one goes ahead with his own meal, and one is hungry and
another is drunk. What! Do you not have houses to eat
and drink in? Or do you despise the church of God and
humiliate those who have nothing? What shall I say to
you? Shall I commend you in this? No, I will not.

For I received from the Lord what I also delivered
to you, that the Lord Jesus on the night when he was
betrayed took bread, and when he had given thanks, he
broke it, and said, "This is my body which is for you. Do
this in remembrance of me." In the same way also the
cup, after the supper, saying, "This cup is the new
covenant in my blood. Do this, as often as you drink it, in
remembrance of me." For as often as you eat this bread
and drink the cup, you proclaim the Lord's death until he
comes.

Whoever, therefore, eats the bread or drinks the cup
of the Lord in an unworthy manner will be guilty of
profaning the body and blood of the Lord. Let a man
examine himself, and so eat of the bread and drink of the

cup. For any one who eats and drinks without discerning
the body eats and drinks judgment upon himself.

1 Corinthians 11:18–29

Paul's rebuke to the congregation at Corinth applies to us,
for among us, too, a dispute has broken out concerning
the Eucharist; among us, too, the opposition of one party
to another threatens to obscure the central mystery of the
Church. In this dispute about the holy Eucharist there are
two parties opposed to each other: the one, let us call them
the progressives, says that with the traditional form of celebrating the Mass the Church has strayed far from the original
intentions of the Lord. The Lord, they say, held a simple meal
of fellowship with his disciples, and he said: "Do this in
remembrance of me!" But it is precisely this that the Church
does not do, they say; rather, she has made of it yet another
sacral cultic ritual; she has reworked the whole thing into the
Mass, has surrounded it with richly decorated cathedrals and
with an imposing and sublime Liturgy, and has thus altered
beyond recognition the simple nature of what Jesus com-
manded us to do. The watchword that emerges from such
reflections is: desacralization. The Lord's Supper should once
more become a simple, human, everyday meal. And from
that there followed, for instance, the conclusion that it is not
really right to have a church building, but we should have a
multipurpose area, so that the Lord's Supper can truly be held
in an everyday setting and not be elevated into a cultic ritual.
In the same way the demand emerged to do away with liturgical forms and vestments and the call to get back to the
way we look in ordinary daily life. The louder these voices
became, and the more such things were actually put into
practice, the more strongly there arose an objection to the
contrary, directed against the liturgical reform as a whole.

The reshaped Liturgy was accused of puritanism, poverty, iconoclasm. It was said that the Mass had been made completely Protestant and that the real Catholic element in it had been destroyed. Thus, it was said, the Catholic Church, at this point in her very heart, had ceased to be catholic. The Eucharist would have to be celebrated outside her and despite her, since there was no longer a valid Eucharist within her. With these things in mind, let us try to look at these two questions.

And now the first question: Jesus did not, it is said, call for any kind of cult or liturgy, but just an everyday meal of fellowship, when he said: "Do *this*!" Plausible though this objection may seem, as soon as we listen more carefully to Holy Scripture and refuse to be satisfied with superficialities, it becomes clear to us that it is untrue. For Jesus did not command his disciples to repeat the Last Supper as such and as a whole; this would in any case not have been possible, as it was a Passover meal.[1] But Passover is an annual festival, with a quite specific date in the lunar calendar, which comes around just once a year. No more than I can keep Christmas whenever I feel like it can the Passover just be continually repeated. Jesus did not give the command to repeat, as a whole, this Jewish liturgy that he had kept with his people— this, as we said, would have been impossible. His command to repeat something referred to the new element he was presenting them, to his gift of himself, which he had instituted within the old setting of the worship of Israel. We are thus

---

[1] The difference between the Johannine and the synoptic Christology supports this; cf. R. Pesch, *Das Markusevangelium*, vol. 2 (Freiburg, 1977), pp. 323–28; R. Schnackenburg, *Das Johannesevangelium*, vol. 3 (Freiburg, 1975), pp. 38–53. Besides this, John assumes the presence of the ritual elements of the Passover meal (Pesch, *Markusevangelium*, 2:326), so that the fact of this being something that could not simply be repeated in the Christian community applies likewise, indeed especially, in his case.

presented with the *essential element*, but it has not yet found a new Christian form. Not until the moment when, through the Cross and the Resurrection and the story that followed, the Church emerged from within Israel as an independent community could this new gift find its own new form. And that gives rise to the question: From what source did the Mass actually derive its shape, if it was not possible to repeat the entire Last Supper as such? What could the disciples build upon to develop this new shape?

Nowadays New Testament scholars essentially give one of two answers. Some of them say that the Eucharist of the early Church built upon meals that Jesus shared with his disciples day after day. Others say that the Eucharist is the *continuation of the meals with sinners* that Jesus had held.[2] This second idea has become for many people a fascinating notion with far-reaching consequences. For it would mean that the Eucharist is the sinners' banquet, where Jesus sits at the table; the Eucharist is the public gesture by which he invites everyone without exception. The logic of this is expressed in a far-reaching criticism of the Church's Eucharist, since it implies that the Eucharist cannot be conditional on anything, not dependent on denomination or even on baptism. It is necessarily an open table to which all may come to encounter the universal God, without any limit or denominational preconditions. But then, again—however tempting the idea may be—it contradicts what we find in the Bible. Jesus' Last Supper was not one of those meals he held with "publicans and sinners". He made it subject to the basic form of the Passover, which implies that this meal was held in a family setting.

---

[2] There are more details on this in my essay, "Gestalt und Gehalt der eucharistischen Feier" [Form and content in the eucharistic celebration], in my *Das Fest des Glaubens*, 3d ed. (Einsiedeln, 1993), pp. 31–54 [English trans., *The Feast of Faith*, trans. Graham Harrison (San Francisco: Ignatius Press, 1986), pp. 33–60].

Thus he kept it with his new family, with the Twelve; with those whose feet he washed, whom he had prepared, by his Word and by this cleansing of absolution (Jn 13:10), to receive a blood relationship with him, to become one body with him.[3] The Eucharist is not itself the sacrament of reconciliation, but in fact it presupposes that sacrament. It is the *sacrament of the reconciled*, to which the Lord invites all those who have become one with him; who certainly still remain weak sinners, but yet have given their hand to him and have become part of his family. That is why, from the beginning, the Eucharist has been preceded by a discernment. We have just heard this, in very dramatic form, from Paul: Whoever eats unworthily, eats and drinks judgment on himself, because he does not distinguish the Body of the Lord (1 Cor 11:27ff.). The *Teaching of the Twelve Apostles*, one of the oldest writings outside the New Testament, from the beginning of the second century, takes up this apostolic tradition and has the priest, just before distributing the Sacrament, saying: "Whoever is holy, let him approach—whoever is not, let him do penance!"[4] The Eucharist is—let us repeat it—the sacrament of those who have let themselves be reconciled by God, who have thus become members of his family and put themselves into his hands. That is why there are conditions for participating in it; it presupposes that we have voluntarily entered into the mystery of Jesus Christ.

Yet even the second line of inquiry to which we referred—

---

[3] Cf. on this point especially John 13:8, which speaks of "having a part" in Jesus, where, on the one hand, we hear an echo of eucharistic terminology, while, on the other, there is a recognizable application to the depths of our being. Cf. Schnackenburg, *Johannesevangelium*, 2:21; R. Bultmann, *Das Evangelium des Johannes*, 15th ed. (Göttingen, 1957), p. 357, n. 3; and there is important material on this subject in K. Hein, *Eucharist and Excommunication: A Study in Early Christian Doctrine and Discipline* (Frankfurt, 1973).

[4] *Didache* 10:6.

supposing that the Eucharist was built upon the *daily fellow-ship meals Jesus held* with his disciples—is unconvincing, since we know that in the first place the Eucharist was celebrated every Sunday; so that it was in fact something apart from ordinary everyday life and thus apart from everyday table fellowship. It was the Resurrection that offered the actual starting point for the Christian shaping of the legacy of Jesus. It was this, basically, that opened up the possibility of his being present beyond the limitations of earthly corporeal existence and of sharing himself out. But the Resurrection took place on the first day of the week. The Jews saw this as the day on which the world was created. For Jesus' disciples, it became the day on which a new world began, the day when, with the breaking of the bonds of death, the new creation had its beginning. It was the day on which Jesus Christ entered the world anew as the Risen One. Thereby he had made this day, the first day of creation, his day, the "Day of the Lord". It is already called that in the first century; that is the name given in the Book of Revelation (1:10). And both in the Acts of the Apostles (20:7) and in the First Letter to the Corinthians (16:2) we find evidence that this was the day of the Eucharist. The Lord had risen on the first day of the week; and this day, his day, was kept week after week as the day of remembrance of the new thing that had happened. In doing this, the disciples had no need to look back on the Resurrection as something in the past: the Risen One is alive; that is why the day of Resurrection was, of its very nature, the day of his presence, the day he gathered them together, when they gathered around him. Sunday, as the day of the Resurrection, became the inner basis, the inner point of location, for the eucharistic celebration of the developing Church. It was on this basis that its shape was developed.

It was now, as it were, transplanted out of the soil of the

Jewish Passover into the context of the Resurrection: its essential characteristic was now that of being the *celebration of the Resurrection*. As early as the beginning of the second century, Ignatius of Antioch refers to Christians as those who "live consistently with Sunday",[5] that is to say, people who live on the basis of the Resurrection, of its presence in the eucharistic celebration. Thus the basis for the reshaping of the eucharistic celebration was established. *After* the earthly meal that satisfied the hunger of the assembled believers, they celebrated with praise and thanksgiving the presence of the death and Resurrection of the Lord. Thus, by an inner logic, the Last Supper developed into a celebration in which joy has its place. It is the Acts of the Apostles, again, that tells us that Christians celebrated the Eucharist with songs of praise, and we know from the fifth chapter of the Letter to the Ephesians (5:19; cf. Col 3:16), and from many other passages, that they praised the Lord with psalms and hymns and songs.[6] By its being transplanted into the context of the Resurrection, without which the Eucharist would be merely the remembrance of a departure with no return, there arose two natural developments: worship and praise, that is to say, its cultic characteristics, and also the joy over the glory of the Risen One.

But the shaping of the Eucharist, the developed form of the Church's Liturgy, was still not completed. We have to bear in mind that Jewish worship had two elements. One was the sacrificial worship in the Temple, where in accordance with what the law prescribed the various sacrifices were offered. Side by side with this Temple worship, which took

---

[5] *Letter to the Magnesians* 9:1.

[6] Cf. E. Peterson, "Von den Engeln" [On angels], in his *Theologische Traktate* (Munich, 1951), pp. 323–407; J. Ratzinger, *Theologische Probleme der Kirchenmusik* (Rottenburg, 1978).

place, and could only take place, in Jerusalem, a second element was steadily developing: the synagogue, which could be set up anywhere. Here the service of the word was celebrated, the Holy Scriptures were read, the Psalms were sung, people joined in praising God, hearing the Word of God interpreted, and making petitions to God. After the Resurrection of Jesus, his followers ceased to take part in the sacrificial cult in the Temple. They could no longer do so, for the curtain in the Temple was torn, that is, the Temple was empty.[7] It was no longer that stone building that was the Temple, but the Lord, who had opened himself to the Father as the living Temple and had opened a way for the Father, from himself, into humanity. In place of the Temple there is the Eucharist, since Christ is the true Paschal Lamb; everything that ever took place in the Temple has been fulfilled in him.

But while, for this reason, the disciples no longer shared in the bloody sacrifices of the Temple but celebrated the *new* Paschal Lamb in their stead, they continued to take part in the synagogue worship just as before. The Bible of Israel was, after all, the Bible of Jesus Christ. They knew that the whole of the Holy Scriptures, law and prophets, was talking about him; they therefore tried to read this holy book of their fathers, together with Israel, as referring to Jesus and thus to open Israel's heart to Jesus. They continued to sing the Psalms with Israel, so as thus to sing them with Jesus, and from within the New Covenant to open up a way to understanding them from the standpoint of Christ. Yet at the same time we can follow, in the texts of the New Testament, that tragic path which was to lead eventually to the breakdown of what

[7] Cf. W. Trilling, *Christusverkündigung in den synoptischen Evangelien* [The proclamation of Christ in the synoptic Gospels] (Munich, 1969), pp. 191–211; Y. Congar, *Le Mystère du temple* (Paris, 1957), pp. 158–80.

remained of unity with Israel. Christians were unable to persuade Israel to read the Bible as the word of Jesus Christ and for Jesus Christ. The synagogue rapidly closed itself against such an interpretation of Holy Scripture, and toward the end of the first century the break was complete. It was no longer possible to understand Scripture in company with Jesus within the synagogue. Thus Israel and the Church stood separate, side by side. The Church had become an independent entity. Since she could now no longer share in Israel's service of the word, she had to perform her own. This meant necessarily that the two halves of the Liturgy, hitherto separate, came together: the service of the Word became united with the eucharistic worship; and now that this had taken on the shape of fully developed Christian worship, and the Church was thus fully the Church, the whole thing was relocated to Sunday morning, the time of the Resurrection; the logic of the Resurrection had worked itself out.

The basic Christian form of worship, as we keep it up to the present day in the Church's Eucharist, was thereby completed. It looks like this: At the beginning is the service of the Word, consisting of readings from the Old and New Testaments, songs from the Psalms, new prayers, and the joyous greeting of the Lord, the Kyrie, which is the transformation of the ancient cry in homage to the emperor into the cry in homage to Christ as the true Lord of the world.[8] There follows the eucharistic worship itself, and in our earlier reflections we saw that the Canon, as an inclusive "Sacrifice of the Word", grew directly out of the prayer of Israel and of Jesus, given substance now with the narrative and action from the Last Supper as its new heart and also with Holy Communion. Thus, out of the inner logic of Jesus' giving of

[8] Theodor Schnitzler, *Was die Messe bedeutet: Hilfen zur Mitfeier* [The meaning of the Mass: Aids to its celebration] (Freiburg, 1976), pp. 73–78.

himself, the shape of the Mass sprang. It developed without any break, as the fulfillment of the original command; and now that it had completed this development, it stood open to receive the wealth of the Temple, the wealth of the nations. Naturally it is always in need of purification. That is the task in every century. And a part of that great process is what we have seen happening, certainly not for the first time, in the middle of our own century. It is always a matter of allowing the wealth of prayers and hopes and faith of all the peoples to find a way in, on one hand, but, on the other, of clearing things away so that its heart is not obscured, so that the mystery of Jesus Christ itself remains visible in its sublime purity. Anyone who has understood that knows that the historical development of the Church's Eucharist is not a decline from its origins but the true fruit of those origins. Those attempts to tell us that we should "get back" to a simple profane meal, to multipurpose areas and so on, are only in appearance a return to the origins. In reality, they are a step back behind the *turning point of the Cross and the Resurrection*, that is, behind the essentials that are the basis for Christianity in all its novelty. This is not restoring the original state, but abandoning the mystery of Easter and, thereby, the very center of the mystery of Christ.

And now we can turn to the second question, which is voiced ever more loudly. Has the fruit of this growth not been destroyed in the reform of the Liturgy? We do not wish to concern ourselves here with particular cases of abuse, which have no doubt occurred and probably are still occurring. On that point I would wish to say only this: We all need to be quite clear that the Eucharist is not at the disposal of any individual priest or that of any particular congregation but is the gift of Jesus Christ to the whole Church, and that it retains its sublime quality only if we accept it as being exempt from arbitrary change. All those apparent successes we are aiming for, if instead we give free rein to our own creations, remain mere show and a pottage of lentils, because they obscure the fact that there is more happening, in the true Eucharist of the Church, than we can ever organize ourselves. So let us talk no more about abuses for which individuals are responsible and which we have to try to overcome through our common faith. Let us talk about the attacks that are made upon the authorized form of the Liturgy. We have already mentioned the dispute about "for many" or "for all", in the first of these reflections.

There are three further substantial objections. One says that with the changes to the Offertory the sacrificial aspect of the Mass has been destroyed and that the Mass has thus ceased to be Catholic. A second is directed against the manner of receiving Communion: standing, in the hand. And of course the question of the language is also still a matter of dispute.

Let us start with the first. A sociologist who teaches at Saarbrücken has tried to show, with a great display of learning, that it is of the essence of any religion, and especially the Catholic religion, that a *sacrifice* be offered.[9] But instead of that, he says, hymns of praise have now been introduced. Thus there is no longer any sacrifice, and since the Council the Eucharist, he suggests, is no longer the Mass of the Catholic Church. Well, even a modest acquaintance with the *Little Catechism* would be enough for us to realize that the sacrificial dimension was never located in the Offertory, but in the Eucharistic Prayer, the Canon. For we do not offer God this or that thing; the new element in the Eucharist is the presence of the sacrifice of *Christ*. Therefore the sacrifice

---

[9] W. Siebel, *Freiheit und Herrschaftsstruktur in der Kirche: Eine soziologische Studie* [Freedom and structural domination in the Church: A sociological study], (Berlin, 1971), pp. 20–52.

is effective where *his* word is heard, the word of the Word, by which he transformed his death into an event of meaning and of love, in order that we, through being able to take up his words for ourselves, are led onward into his love, onward into the love of the Trinity, in which he eternally hands himself over to the Father. There, where the words of the Word ring forth, and our gifts thus become his gifts, through which he gives himself, *that* is the sacrificial element that has ever and always been characteristic of the Eucharist.

What we call the "Offertory" has another significance.[10] The German word *Opferung*, and likewise the English word "offertory", comes either from the Latin *offerre*, or more probably from *operare*.[11] *Offerre* does not mean to sacrifice (that is *immolare* in Latin); it is rather to provide, prepare, make available.[12] And *operari* means to effect; in this case it, too, means to prepare. The idea was simply that at this point the eucharistic altar had to be made ready and that to this end *operari*, that is, various activity, was necessary, so that the candles, the gifts, bread and wine, should be standing ready for the Eucharist, as was befitting. This was therefore in the first instance simply an external preparation for what was to happen. But people very soon came to understand it in a deeper sense. They borrowed the action of the head of the household in Judaism, who holds the bread up before the face of

---

[10] There is a widespread misunderstanding among many German speakers, who have been misled by the verbal similarity between *Opfer* (= "sacrifice") and *Opferung* (= "offertory"); Cardinal Ratzinger is here trying to unravel this confusion.—TRANS.

[11] Schnitzler, *Was die Messe bedeutet*, pp. 117ff.

[12] Concerning the semantic field of *offerre*, see the important study of R. Berger, *Die Wendung "offerre pro" in der römischen Liturgie* [The expression *offerre pro* in the Roman Liturgy] (Münster, 1965); cf. also on this point J. A. Jungmann, *Messe im Gottesvolk: Eine nachkonziliarer Durchblick durch Missarum Sollemnia* [The Mass amidst God's people: A look at *Missarum Sollemnia* in the light of the Council] (Freiburg, 1970), pp. 60–67.

God, so as to receive it anew from him. By lifting up the gifts to God, by entering together into Israel's manner of preparing itself for God, the outward acts of preparation were increasingly understood as an inward preparation for the approach of God, who seeks us out himself through our gifts. Right up to the ninth or tenth century this act of preparation, which had been taken over from Israel, happened without any words. Then there arose a feeling that every action in the Christian sphere also required words. Thus in about the tenth century those offertory prayers were composed that the older ones among us know and love from the old missal and perhaps even miss in the new form of Mass. These prayers were beautiful and profound. But we have to admit that they carried within them the seeds of a certain misunderstanding. The way they were formulated always looked forward to the actual matter of the Canon. Both elements, the preparation and the actual sacrifice of Christ, were intertwined in these words. Something that made good sense within the world of faith, and within the faith can be understood—that is, that in our approach to Christ we are always carried onward by his coming to find us—was also liable, for those looking on from outside or those who came seeking the truth, to lead to misunderstanding. That it did have this effect is shown by the reactions we were just talking about.

For this reason, those who were reforming the Liturgy wished first of all to return to the situation before the ninth century and to leave the ritual of offering the gifts without any words. The Holy Father, Pope Paul VI, decided personally, and with some emphasis, that some words of prayer would have to remain here. He himself took part in the formulation of these prayers. In their main outlines they are derived from the table prayers of Israel. We must also bear in mind that all these prayers over meals of Israel, these blessings, as they are called, are related to the Paschal Mystery; they look toward the Passover of Israel, are thought out on that basis and draw their life from it. That means that they are implicitly looking forward to the Paschal Mystery of Jesus Christ, that we may call them at the same time both Advent and Easter prayers. Above all, we will recall that the Holy Family, Jesus, Mary, and Joseph, prayed in this way—on their flight into Egypt, in the strange land, and then at home in Nazareth, and again that Jesus prayed in this way with his disciples. At that time the Jewish rule was probably already in force that in the evening the mother lights the candles and that she is then the leader of family prayers. Thus, in these prayers we may hear the voice of Mary and pray with her. The whole secret life of Nazareth, this Advent progression toward the Easter event, is present in them. Thus, a new treasure has entered the Liturgy. We start, as it were, with Nazareth, in the act of preparation, and from there we move—in the middle of the Canon—toward Golgotha, and finally on into the Resurrection event of Communion.[13] I think if we hear these new old prayers in this way, then they can become for us a wonderful treasure in uniting us with the earthly life of Jesus, uniting us with the waiting prayer of Israel, and in our sharing the journey from Nazareth to Golgotha and up to the hour of the Resurrection.

The second objection we wanted to consider was directed against the act of receiving Communion: *kneeling—standing, hand—mouth*. Well, first of all, I would like to say that both attitudes are possible, and I would like therefore to ask all priests to exercise tolerance and to recognize the decision of each person; and I would further like to ask you all to exercise

---

[13] Cf. on this whole matter the fine expositions in Schnitzler, *Was die Messe bedeutet*, pp. 117–29, especially pp. 122f.; and in L. Bouyer, *Woman in the Church*, trans. Marilyn Teichert (San Francisco: Ignatius Press, 1979), p. 19.

the same tolerance and not to cast aspersions on anyone who may have opted for this or that way of doing it. But you will ask: Is tolerance the proper answer here? Or is it not misplaced with respect to this most holy thing? Well, here again we know that until the ninth century Communion was received in the hand, standing. That does not of course mean that it should always be so. For what is fine, sublime, about the Church is that she is growing, maturing, understanding the mystery more profoundly. In that sense the new development that began after the ninth century is quite justified, as an expression of reverence, and is well-founded. But, on the other hand, we have to say that the Church could not possibly have been celebrating the Eucharist unworthily for nine hundred years.

If we read what the Fathers say, we can see in what a spirit of reverence they received Communion. We find a particularly fine passage in the writings of Cyril of Jerusalem, from the fourth century. In his catechetical homilies he tells the candidates for baptism what they should do at Communion. They should make a throne of their hands, laying the right upon the left to form a throne for the King, forming at the same time a cross. This symbolic gesture, so fine and so profound, is what concerns him: the hands of man form a cross, which becomes a throne, down into which the King inclines himself. The open, outstretched hand can thus become a sign of the way that a man offers himself to the Lord, opens his hands for him, that they may become an instrument of his presence and a throne of his mercies in this world.[14] Anyone

---

[14] *Mystagogical Catechesis* 5:21, ed. A. Piédagnel, Sources chrétiennes, no. 126 (1966), pp. 170ff.; revised and introduced by G. Röwekamp, Fontes Christiani, vol. 7 (Freiburg, 1992), pp. 162f.; cf. J. A. Jungmann, *Missarum Sollemnia*, vol. 2 (Freiburg, 1952), p. 469, and, regarding the ritual form of the Communion of the faithful in history, pp. 463–86.

who reflects on this will recognize that on this point it is quite wrong to argue about this or that form of behavior. We should be concerned only to argue in favor of what the Church's efforts were directed toward, both before and after the ninth century, that is, a reverence in the heart, an inner submission before the mystery of God that puts himself into our hands. Thus we should not forget that not only our hands are impure but also our tongue and also our heart and that we often sin more with the tongue than with the hands. God takes an enormous risk—and at the same time this is an expression of his merciful goodness—in allowing not only our hand and our tongue but even our heart to come into contact with him. We see this in the Lord's willingness to enter into us and live with us, within us, and to become from within the heart of our life and the agent of its transformation.

And finally allow me to say just a few words about *language*. Here again there are two points to consider, which between them open the possibility of a whole range of varying decisions and practice. On one hand, using the magnificent terminology of Hellenistic culture, the Roman Canon calls the action of the Mass *rationabile obsequium*—an action of the word, an action in which spirit and reason play their part. The Word of God wants to speak to man, wants to be understood and answered by him. That is why in Rome, in about the third century, when Greek was no longer generally understood, they made the transition from Greek, which had hitherto been used in the Eucharist, to Latin.[15] But there is also a second point. The Church later hesitated to make use of the developing national languages of Europe in the Liturgy, first of all, because for a long time they had not attained the literary level or the unity of usage that would have permitted a

---

[15] Cf. Theodor Klauser, *Kleine Abendländische Liturgiegeschichte* [A brief history of Western Liturgy] (Bonn, 1965), pp. 23–28.

common celebration of the Eucharist over a wide area; but then also because she was opposed to anything that would give a national identity to this mystery, because she wanted to express in the language, too, the inclusive character that reaches out beyond the boundaries of place and time. She was able to keep on with Latin as the common liturgical language because she knew that, while it is, in the Eucharist, *also* a matter of comprehensibility, yet it is more than comprehensibility—that this demands a greater, more mature, and more inclusive understanding than that of mere comprehension: she knew that, here, the heart must also understand.

After what we have said, use of the vernacular is in principle justified. It would be a danger only if it were to drag the Eucharist back into the realm of national culture. It would be a danger only if we were to push our translation to the point where only what was immediately comprehensible or, even, obvious in everyday terms remained. In any such translation you would have to omit more and more, until the essential meaning disappeared. Because things are as they are, we should gratefully accept both: the normal form of Eucharist is in the vernacular, but we should not on that account forget to pray it, to love it, in the common language of the Church over the centuries, so that in this unsettled and changeable world, in which the nations are forever meeting and mingling with each other, we are still able ever and again to worship together and, in that language, to praise the living God together. Here too, we should rise above a fruitless dispute and become one in the multiplicity the Lord has given us; one in recognizing and in loving the understanding and comprehensibility but also the inclusiveness that transcends the rationality of what is immediately understood.

Let me now, to finish, tell you a little story about Martin Buber. The value of understanding things clearly is apparent in it; but at the same time it is marvelously persuasive for the greater possibilities of an understanding heart. Martin Buber tells how Rabbi Levi Yitzhak of Berdichev came one day to an inn where many merchants were staying overnight. In the morning they said morning prayers. It turned out that there was only one phylactery, which is what one must put on, according to Jewish tradition, to say the morning prayers. So this was handed from one to the other, and because that was taking so much time, each one, out of consideration for his neighbor, said the prayers so quickly that you could hardly catch a single distinct word of them. The Rabbi, watching this, felt increasingly uncomfortable; and when the whole thing was over, he turned to two young people and just said to them, "Ma-ma-ma, wa-wa-wa." They looked at him in amazement and said, "What is it you want?" In reply, he said again just "Ma-ma-ma, wa-wa-wa." At this, they took him— quite understandably—for an idiot. But he said to them, "Do you really not understand that language, when you've just been talking to the Lord God in it?" After a moment of confusion, one of them said, "Have you never seen a child lying in a cradle, who doesn't yet know how to talk properly? Haven't you heard how he makes all sorts of noises with his mouth: Ma-ma-ma, wa-wa-wa? All the wise men and scholars together cannot understand what he says; but when his mother comes, she knows straight away what the noises mean." [16] This story is not an argument in favor of baby talk. But it does make us aware that there is an understanding of the heart that reaches beyond a literal understanding. We should seek above all for this understanding of the heart, so that our words may be filled with life and we may worthily praise the living God.

[16] Martin Buber, *Werke*, vol. 3, *Schriften zum Chassidismus* [Writings on Hasidism] (Munich and Freiburg, 1963), p. 334.

The Presence of the Lord
in the Sacrament

The Real Presence of Christ in the Eucharistic Sacrament

Jesus said: "I am the bread of life. Your fathers ate the manna in the wilderness, and they died. This is the bread which comes down from heaven, that a man may eat of it and not die. I am the living bread which came down from heaven; if any one eats of this bread, he will live for ever; and the bread which I shall give for the life of the world is my flesh."

The Jews then disputed among themselves, saying, "How can this man give us his flesh to eat?" So Jesus said to them, "Truly, truly, I say to you, unless you eat the flesh of the Son of man and drink his blood, you have no life in you; he who eats my flesh and drinks my blood has eternal life, and I will raise him up at the last day. For my flesh is food indeed, and my blood is drink indeed. He who eats my flesh and drinks my blood abides in me, and I in him. As the living Father sent me, and I live because of the Father, so he who eats me will live because of me. This is the bread which came down from heaven, not such as the Fathers ate and died; he who eats this bread will live for ever." Jesus said this in the synagogue, as he taught at Capernaum.   —John 6:48–59

Saint Thomas Aquinas, in his sermon for Corpus Christi, picked up the saying from the fifth book of Moses, which expresses Israel's joy over its election, over the mystery of the covenant. The saying goes: "What great nation is there that has a god so near to it as the LORD our God is to us?" (Deut 4:7).[1] We can sense, in Thomas' words, a tone of triumphant joy at the way this saying from the Old Testament had acquired its true sublimity only in the Church, in God's new people. For if, in Israel, God had humbled himself in his speaking to Moses, and had thus drawn near to his people, now he himself has taken flesh, has become a man among men, and has remained, so far remained that he places himself, in the mystery of transubstantiated bread, in our hands and in our hearts. This joy at the way that a "people of God" has truly come into being, that God is so near that he could be no closer, was the origin in the thirteenth century of the Feast of Corpus Christi, as one great hymn of thanksgiving that such a thing could be.

But we all know that something that is in fact a cause for rejoicing, and rightly so, is at the same time a stumbling block, a crisis point, and was so from the beginning. For we have heard, in the reading from the Gospel of John, how at the very first advance notice concerning the Eucharist people murmured and revolted against it. Since that time, the murmurs have run down through the centuries, and in particular the Church of our own generation has been deeply hurt by them. We do not want God as near as that; we do not want him so small, humbling himself; we want him to be great and far away. Thus questions arise, which are intended to show that his coming so near is impossible. If, in this meditation, we reflect on a couple of these questions, it is not a matter of indulging a taste for difficulties, but in order to learn anew and more profoundly the Yes of faith, to receive anew its joy

---

[1] Thomas Aquinas, *Officium de festo Corporis Christi*, in *Sanctae Thomae Aquinatis Opera Omnia*, ed. R. Busa, S.J. (Stuttgart and Bad Canstatt, 1980), 6:581 = DSG ps. 3, n. 3; ps. 5, n. 3.

and thus to learn anew once more to pray and to know the Eucharist itself. There are three questions above all that are opposed to the belief in the real presence of the Lord. The first: Does the Bible actually say anything like that? Does it present us with this, or is it just the naïve misunderstanding of a later age, which transposed the exalted and spiritual reality of Christianity down to a lesser ecclesiastical version? The second question is this: Is it truly possible for a body to share itself out into all places and all times? Does this not simply contradict the limitations that are of the essence of a body? The third question is: Hasn't modern science, with everything it says about "substance" and material being, so obviously rendered obsolete those dogmas of the Church that relate to this that in the world of science we just finally have to throw them on the scrap heap, since we are unable to reconcile them with contemporary thought?

Let us turn to the first question: Does the Bible say anything like that? We know that in the sixteenth century this dispute was passionately pursued as a dispute about one word, about "is": "This is my Body, this is my Blood." Does this "is" really signify the full force of bodily presence? Or does it not merely indicate an image, so that it should be understood: "This stands for my Body and my Blood"? In the meantime scholars have disputed about this word until they were weary of it and have realized that an argument about a single word, removed from its context, can only lead up a blind alley. For just as in music a note derives its significance from the interrelating whole, and can only be understood within the whole, so also we can only understand the words in a sentence by the meaning of the whole within which they have their place. We must ask about the whole context. If we do that, the Bible gives a perfectly clear answer. We have just heard the dramatic and incomparably explicit words of Jesus from John's Gospel: "Unless you eat the flesh of the Son of man and drink his blood, you have no life in you. . . . My flesh is food indeed" (6:53, 55). When the murmuring of the Jews arose, the controversy could easily have been quieted by the assurance: Friends, do not be disturbed; this was only metaphorical language; the flesh only signifies food, it isn't actually that!—But there is nothing of that in the Gospel. Jesus renounces any such toning down; he just says with renewed emphasis that this bread has to be literally, physically eaten. He says that faith in the God who became man is believing in a God with a body and that this faith is real and fulfilled; it brings full union only if it is itself corporeal, if it is a sacramental event in which the corporeal Lord seizes hold of our bodily existence. In order to express fully the intensity and reality of this fusion, Paul compares what happens in Holy Communion with the physical union between man and woman. To help us understand the Eucharist, he refers us to the words in the creation story: "The two [= man and wife] shall become one" (Gen 2:24). And he adds: "He who is united to the Lord becomes one spirit [that is, shares a single new existence in the Holy Spirit] with him" (1 Cor 6:17).

When we hear this, we at once have some notion of how the presence of Jesus Christ is to be understood. It is not something at rest but is a power that catches us up and works to draw us within itself.[2] Augustine had a profound grasp of

---

[2] Most insistent on the Real Presence in Paul's writings is E. Käsemann, "Anliegen und Eigenart der paulinischen Abendmahlslehre" [The concerns and characteristics of Paul's teaching on the Lord's Supper], in his *Exegetische Versuche und Besinnungen*, vol. 1 (Göttingen, 1960), pp. 11–34; on p. 28, as a summary of the preceding analysis: "The expression 'Real Presence', therefore, whatever objection may be raised against it, exactly expresses what Paul means." On John 6, see: H. Schlier, "Johannes 6 und das johanneische Verständnis der Eucharistie" [John 6 and the Johannine understanding of the Eucharist], in his *Das Ende der Zeit* (Freiburg, 1971), pp. 102–23.

this in his teaching on Communion. In the period before his conversion, when he was struggling with the incarnational aspect of Christian belief, which he found impossible to approach from the point of view of Platonic idealism, he had a sort of vision, in which he heard a voice saying to him: "I am the bread of the strong, eat me! But you will not transform me and make me part of you; rather, I will transform you and make you part of me."[3] In the normal process of eating, the human is the stronger being. He takes things in, and they are assimilated into him, so that they become part of his own substance. They are transformed within him and go to build up his bodily life. But in the mutual relation with Christ it is the other way around; he is the heart, the truly existent being. When we truly communicate, this means that we are taken out of ourselves, that we are assimilated into him, that we become one with him and, through him, with the fellowship of our brethren.

And now we have already arrived at our second question: Is it really possible for a body to share itself out so that it is many hosts, so that beyond the limits of place and time this body is always there? Now, we certainly have to be quite aware, first of all, that we will never wholly understand something like that, since what is happening is part of God's sphere, the sphere of the Resurrection. We, however, do not live in the sphere of the Resurrection. We live on the hither side of death's boundary. If we could perhaps imagine some creature that did not have three dimensions, height, length, and breadth, but only two, in a flat plane, then such a being would never be able to imagine a third dimension, simply because it does not have such a dimension itself. It would only be able to try to think beyond its own limitations, but without ever

[3] Augustine, *Confessions*, bk. 7, 10:16.

really being able to picture this other thing or fully to comprehend it. That is just how it is with us. We live in the sphere of death; we can reach out in thought into the sphere of the Resurrection, try to make approximations. But it remains something different that we never quite comprehend. This is because of the boundary of death, which closes us in and within which we live.

But we can look for approximations. One of these becomes apparent when we reflect that in the language of the Bible the word "body"—"This is my Body"—does not mean just a body, in contradistinction to the spirit, for instance. Body, in the language of the Bible, denotes rather the whole person, in whom body and spirit are indivisibly one. "This is my Body" therefore means: This is my whole person, existent in bodily form. What the nature of this person is, however, we learn from what is said next: "which is given up for you". That means: This person is: existing-for-others. It is in its most intimate being a sharing with others. But that is why, since it is a matter of this person and because it is from its heart an opening up, a self-giving person, it can then be shared out.

We can understand that a little bit, just from the experience of our own bodily existence. When we reflect on what the body means for us, we will notice that it carries within it a certain contradiction. On the one hand, the body is the boundary that separates us from others. Where this body is, no other body can be. When I am in this place, I am not at the same time elsewhere. Thus the body is the boundary that separates us from each other; and it thus involves our being somehow strangers to each other. We cannot look inside the other person; corporeal existence hides his inner self; he remains hidden from us; on that account, indeed, we are strangers even to ourselves. We cannot even see into ourselves, into our own depths. That is one thing, then: The body is a boundary that makes us opaque, impermeable for each other, which sets us beside each other and prevents our being able to see or to touch each other's intimate selves. But there is a second thing: The body is also a bridge. For we meet each other through the body; through it we communicate in the common material of creation; through it we can see ourselves, feel ourselves, come close to one another. In the gestures of the body are revealed who and what the other person is. We see ourselves in the way the body sees, looks, acts, offers itself; it leads us to each other: it is both boundary and means of communion in one.

That is why anyone can live out his bodily existence in different ways: we can live it out more inclined toward shutting off or more inclined toward communion. A person can live his bodily existence, and within it the existence of himself, so much directed toward shutting off, toward selfishness, that it becomes hardly more than a boundary and no longer opens up meetings with others. Then comes about what Albert Camus once depicted as the tragic situation of men in relation to each other: It is as if two people are separated by the glass wall of a telephone box. They can see each other; they are quite close; and yet there is this wall that keeps them apart. Indeed, it seems like frosted glass, which only allows us to see outlines. Man can therefore live in the direction of "body"; he can so shut himself up in selfishness that the body is nothing more than a division, a limit, preventing any communion, and he no longer really encounters anyone in it, lets no one touch his closed-up inner self.

But bodily existence can also be lived in the opposite way: as opening oneself up, as the developing freedom of a person who shares himself. We all know that this happens, too; that transcending the limits we touch one another intimately, are close to each other. What people call telepathy is only an extreme case of what to a lesser extent happens among us all: a hidden movement from the heart, being close to each other even at a distance. Resurrection means quite simply that the body ceases to be a limit and that its capacity for communion remains. Jesus could rise from the dead, and did rise from the dead, because he had become, as the Son and as the One who loved on the Cross, the One who shares himself wholly with others. To have risen from the dead means to be communicable; it signifies being the one who is open, who gives himself. And on that basis we can understand that Jesus, in the speech about the Eucharist that John has handed down to us, puts the Resurrection and the Eucharist together and that the Fathers say that the Eucharist is the medicine of immortality.[4] Receiving Communion means entering into communion with Jesus Christ; it signifies moving into the open through him who alone could overcome the limits and thus, with him and on the basis of his existence, becoming capable of resurrection oneself.

Yet, a further point follows from this. What is given us here is not a piece of a body, not a thing, but him, the Resurrected one himself—the person who shares himself with us in his love, which runs right through the Cross. This means that receiving Communion is always a personal act. It is never merely a ritual performed in common, which we can just pass off as we do with other social routines. In Communion I enter into the Lord, who is communicating himself to me. Sacramental Communion must therefore always be also spiritual Communion. That is why the Liturgy changes over, before Communion, from the liturgical "we" to "I".[5] This

---

[4] Ignatius of Antioch, *Letter to the Ephesians* 20:2.
[5] Cf. on this point the fine article by K. Lehmann, "Persönliches Gebet in der Eucharistiefeier" [Personal prayer in the Eucharist], *Internationale katholische Zeitschrift Communio* 6 (1977): 401–66.

makes demands on me personally. At this point I have to move out, go toward him, call to him. The eucharistic fellowship of the Church is not a collectivity, in which fellowship is achieved by leveling down to the lowest common denominator, but fellowship is created precisely by our each being ourself. It does not rest on the suppression of the self, on collectivization, but arises through our truly setting out, with our whole self, and entering into this new fellowship of the Lord. That is the only way that something other than collectivization can come about; the only way that a true attitude of turning toward each other, one that reaches down to the roots and into the heart and up to the highest level of a person, can develop. Because this is so, the personal approach to Christ, the "I" prayer, is the first part of Communion; that is why we need a time of silence afterward, in which we converse quite personally with the Lord, who is with us. In recent decades, perhaps, we have all far too much lost the habit of this. We have discovered anew the congregation, Liturgy as a communal celebration, and this is a great thing. But we also have to discover anew that fellowship requires the person. We must learn anew this quiet prayer before Communion and the silent time at one with the Lord, abandoning ourselves to him.

And finally a further point becomes obvious: What we receive is—as we were just saying—a person. But this Person is the Lord Jesus Christ, both God and man. The previous devotional understanding of Communion, in earlier centuries, perhaps forgot the man Jesus too much and thought too much about God. But we are in danger of the opposite, of only seeing the man Jesus and forgetting that in him, as he gives himself to us in bodily form, we are at the same time coming into contact with the living God. Yet because this is so, Communion is therefore always simultaneously adoration.

In any genuine human love there is an element of bowing down before the God-given dignity of the other person, who is in the image of God. Even genuine human love cannot mean that we have the other person all to ourselves and possess him; it includes our reverential recognition of something sublime and unique in this other person, whom we can never entirely possess, our bowing down and thus becoming one with him. In our Communion with Jesus Christ this attains a new level, since it inevitably goes beyond any human partnership. The Word of the Lord as our "partner" explains a great deal but leaves much else undisclosed. We are not on the same footing. He is the wholly other; it is the majesty of the living God that comes to us with him. Uniting ourselves with him means submitting and opening ourselves up to his greatness. That has found expression in the devotional approach to Communion in every age. Augustine says in one place, in a sermon to his new communicants: No one can receive Communion without first adoring. Theodore of Mopsuestia, a contemporary of his who was active in Syria, tells us that every communicant, before receiving the holy gift, spoke a word of adoration. What we are told about the monks of Cluny, around the year one thousand, is particularly striking. Whenever they went to receive Communion, they took their shoes off. They knew that the burning bush was here, the mystery before which Moses, in the desert, sank to his knees.[6] The form may change, but what has to remain is the spirit of adoration, which signifies a genuine act of stepping outside ourselves, communication, freeing ourselves from our own selves and thereby in fact discovering human fellowship.

Let us come to the third and last question: Has the teaching about the Real Presence of Christ in the eucharistic gifts

---

[6] These texts are to be found in: J. A. Jungmann, *Missarum Sollemnia* (Freiburg, 1952), 2:467f.

not long been refuted, rendered obsolete, by science? Has the Church not, with her concept of substance—for she speaks of "transubstantiation"—fettered herself, to far too great an extent, to a science that is basically primitive and obsolete? Do we not know precisely how material is constituted: made up of atoms, and these of elementary particles? That bread is not a "substance", and, in consequence, none of the rest of it can possibly be true? Well, objections like that are in the end very superficial. We cannot consider them in detail now, and it certainly is not necessary for each person always to think through every intellectual point that is grappled with in the Church. What matters is that the framework of thought is still intact, for it helps us to live out joyfully, without anxiety, the real heart of the faith that it supports. So let me just point out a couple of things. First: the word "substance" was used by the Church precisely to avoid the naïveté associated with what we can touch or measure. In the twelfth century the mystery of the Eucharist was on the point of being torn apart by two groups, who each in its own way failed to grasp the heart of it. There were those filled with the thought: Jesus is really there. But "reality", for them, was simply physical, bodily. Consequently, they arrived at the conclusion: In the Eucharist we chew on the flesh of the Lord; but therein they were under the sway of a serious misapprehension. For Jesus has risen. We do not eat flesh, as cannibals would do. That is why others quite rightly opposed them, arguing against such primitive "realism". But they, too, had fallen into the same fundamental error of regarding only what is material, tangible, visible as reality. They said: Since Christ cannot be there in a body we can bite on, the Eucharist can only be a symbol of Christ; the bread can only signify the body, but not be the body. A dispute such as that has helped the Church to develop a more profound understanding of reality.

After wrestling with the difficulty, the insight was made explicit: "Reality" is not just what we can measure. It is not only "quantums", quantifiable entities, that are real; on the contrary, these are always only manifestations of the hidden mystery of true being. But here, where Christ meets us, we have to do with this true being. This is what was being expressed with the word "substance".[7] This does not refer to the quantums, but to the profound and fundamental basis of being. Jesus is not there like a piece of meat, not in the realm of what can be measured and quantified. Anyone who conceives of reality as being like that is deceiving himself about it and about himself. He is living his life all wrong. That is why this is no scholarly dispute but something that affects us ourselves: How should we relate to reality? What is "real"? What should we be like, so as to correspond to what is true? Concerning the Eucharist it is said to us: The substance is transformed, that is to say, the fundamental basis of its being. That is what is at stake, and not the superficial category, to which everything we can measure or touch belongs. Having thought that out, we have taken a good step forward but have still not yet got there. For we now know what is not meant, but the question remains: How is this to be understood, in a positive sense? Again, we will just point out a couple of things, for the limitations of our perception will only allow us hesitant ventures toward this mystery.

a. First. What has always mattered to the Church is that a real transformation takes place here. Something genuinely

---

[7] On transubstantiation, see J. A. Sayes, *La presencía real de Christo en la Eucharistia*, BAC 386 (Madrid, 1976); E. Schillebeeckx, *Die eucharistische Gegenwart* [The eucharistic presence] (Düsseldorf, 1967); A. Gerken, *Theologie der Eucharistie* (Munich, 1973); J. Betz, "Eucharistie als zentrales Mysterium", in J. Feiner and M. Löhrer, *Mysterium Salutis*, vol. 4, no. 2 (Einsiedeln, 1973), pp. 185–311, esp. pp. 289–311; J. Wohlmuth, *Realpräsenz und Transsubstantiation im Konzil von Trient*, two vols. (Frankfurt, 1975).

happens in the Eucharist. There is something new there that was not before. Knowing about a transformation is part of the most basic eucharistic faith. Therefore it cannot be the case that the Body of Christ comes to add itself to the bread, as if bread and Body were two similar things that could exist as two "substances", in the same way, side by side. Whenever the Body of Christ, that is, the risen and bodily Christ, comes, he is greater than the bread, other, not of the same order. The transformation happens, which affects the gifts we bring by taking them up into a higher order and changes them, even if we cannot measure what happens. When material things are taken into our body as nourishment, or for that matter whenever any material becomes part of a living organism, it remains the same, and yet as part of a new whole it is itself changed.[8] Something similar happens here. The Lord takes possession of the bread and the wine; he lifts them up, as it were, out of the setting of their normal existence into a new order; even if, from a purely physical point of view, they remain the same, they have become profoundly different.

That has an important consequence, which at the same time demonstrates more clearly what is meant here: Wherever Christ has been present, afterward it cannot be just as if nothing had happened. There, where he has laid his hand, something new has come to be. This points us back again to the fact that being a Christian as such is to be transformed, that it must involve repentance and not just some embellishment added onto the rest of one's life. It reaches down into our depths and renews us from those very depths. The more we ourselves as Christians are renewed from the root up, the better we can understand the mystery of transformation. Finally, this capacity things have for being transformed makes us

---

[8] Cf. J. Monod, *Zufall und Notwendigkeit: Philosophische Fragen der modernen Biologie*, 5th ed. (Munich, 1973), pp. 79–123.

more aware that the world itself can be transformed, that it will one day as a whole be the New Jerusalem, the Temple, vessel of the presence of God.

b. The second thing is this: What is going on in the Eucharist is an event happening to the thing itself and not just something agreed among ourselves. If the latter were true, then the Eucharist would be merely something arranged among us, a fiction by which we agreed to regard "this" as "something else". Then it would be only a game, not reality. The celebration would be only a kind of game. The gifts would be only temporarily, for cultic purposes, subject to a "change of use". On the contrary: what is happening here is not a "change of use" but a genuine transformation; the Church calls it transubstantiation. Here we are touching on a dispute that raised great waves in the sixties. Then, it was said that we should understand the Eucharist roughly like this: Let us suppose we had a piece of cloth that is made into a national flag or perhaps a regimental flag. It has remained the same cloth, but because this piece of cloth has now become the symbol of a nation or the symbol of a regiment, I have to take my hat off to it. It is not a different thing, but it means something different. Later it will be preserved in a museum and will represent, will carry within it, the whole history of that period. People called the alteration in the cloth transignification, in English, a change of meaning, "change of use". Well, an example like that can certainly help us to understand to a certain extent how being taken into a new context can effect a change.[9] But that

[9] On the theories concerning transfinalization and transignification, see Sayes, *Presencia*, pp. 192–274; J. Wohlmuth, *Realpräsenz*, esp. 1:4–52 and 453–61; W. Beinert, "Die Enzyklika "Mysterium Fidei" und neue Auffassungen über die Eucharistie" [The encyclical "Mysterium Fiedei" and new concepts applied to the Eucharist], *Theologische Quartalschrift* 147 (1967): 159–77. The comparison with a piece of cloth made into a flag had first been formulated by B. Welte

example is inadequate. What happens to bread and wine in the Eucharist is more profound; it is more than a change of use. The Eucharist transcends the realm of functionality.

That is in fact the poverty of our age, that we now think and live only in terms of function, that man himself is classi- fied according to his function, and that we can all be no more than functions and officials, where being is denied. The sig- nificance of the Eucharist as a sacrament of faith consists precisely in that it takes us out of functionality and reaches the basis of reality. The world of the Eucharist is no game; it does not rest on conventions, to which we agree and which we can also renounce; but here it is a matter of reality, of its fundamental basis. That is the crucial point, when the Church rejects mere "change of use" ("transignification") as inad- equate and insists on "change of substance": The Eucharist is more real than the things we have to do with every day. Here is the genuine reality. This is the yardstick, the heart of things; here we encounter that reality against which we need to learn to measure every other reality.

c. Consequent on that is a third thing. If that is how it is, that is, if we do not just change the use of the bread and wine, but through the faithful prayer of the Church the Lord himself is acting and doing a new thing, then that means that his presence remains. It is because it remains, that we adore the Lord in the Host. There are many objections to that. It is said that this was not done during the first thousand years. On that point we must first say simply that the Church grows and matures in the course of history. And we must add that she did already reserve the holy elements, to take them to the sick. This was done on account of knowing that the presence

(in M. Schmaus, *Aktuelle Fragen der Eucharistie* [Current questions concerning the Eucharist] [Munich, 1960]), but for the purposes of an argument that went well beyond questions of function and was ontological in its aim.

of the Lord remains. That is why she has always surrounded the elements with holy reverence.

A second objection goes: The Lord gave himself in bread and wine. Those are things we eat. He showed thereby clearly enough what he meant to happen and what he did not. Accordingly it was said that the bread is there, not to be gazed upon, but to be eaten. This is essentially right: even the Council of Trent says so.[10] But let us just recall: What does that mean, to receive the Lord? That is never just a physical, bodily act, as when I eat a slice of bread. So it can therefore never be something that happens just in a moment. To receive Christ means: to move toward him, to adore him. For that reason, the reception can stretch out beyond the time of the eucharistic celebration; indeed, it has to do so. The more the Church grew into the eucharistic mystery, the more she understood that she could not consummate the celebration of Communion within the limited time available in the Mass. When, thus, the eternal light was lit in the Church, and the tabernacle installed beside the altar, then it was as if the bud of the mystery had opened, and the Church had welcomed the fullness of the eucharistic mystery. The Lord is always there. The church is not just a space in which something sometimes happens early in the morning, while for the rest of the day it stands empty, "unused". There is always the "Church" in the church building, because the Lord is always giving himself, because the eucharistic mystery remains present, and because we, in approaching it, are always included in the worship of the whole believing, praying, and loving Church.

We all know what a difference there is between a church that is always prayed in and one that has become a museum.

[10] Denzinger-Hünermann, no. 643.

There is a great danger today of our churches becoming
museums and suffering the fate of museums: if they are not
locked, they are looted. They are no longer alive. The measure of life in the Church, the measure of her inner open-
ness, will be seen in that she will be able to keep her doors
open, because she is a praying Church. I ask you all therefore from the heart, let us make a new start at this. Let us
again recollect that the Church is always alive, that within
her evermore the Lord comes to meet us. The Eucharist,
and its fellowship, will be all the more complete, the more
we prepare ourselves for him in silent prayer before the
eucharistic presence of the Lord, the more we truly receive
Communion. Adoration such as that is always more than just
talking with God in a general way. But against that could
then rightly be voiced the objection that is always to be
heard: I can just as well pray in the forest, in the freedom of
nature. Certainly, anyone can. But if it were only a matter
of that, then the initiative in prayer would lie entirely with
us; then God would be a mental hypothesis—whether he
answers, whether he can answer or wants to, would remain
open. The Eucharist means, God has answered: The Eucharist is God as an answer, as an answering presence. Now the
initiative no longer lies with us, in the God–man relationship, but with him, and it now becomes really serious. That
is why, in the sphere of eucharistic adoration, prayer attains
a new level; now it is two-way, and so now it really is a
serious business. Indeed, it is now not just two-way, but all-
inclusive: whenever we pray in the eucharistic presence, we
are never alone. Then the whole of the Church, which
celebrates the Eucharist, is praying with us. Then we are
praying within the sphere of God's gracious hearing, because
we are praying within the sphere of death and resurrection,
that is, where the real petition in all our petitions has been

heard: the petition for the victory over death; the petition for the love that is stronger than death.[11]

In this prayer we no longer stand before an imagined God but before the God who has truly given himself to us; before the God who has become for us Communion and who thus frees us and draws us from the margin into communion and leads us on to resurrection. We have to seek again this kind of prayer. The fruit of Lent should be that we become once more a praying Church and, thereby, an open Church. Only the praying Church is open. Only she is alive and invites people in; she offers them fellowship and at the same time a place of silence.

From all these reflections there naturally follows one last consideration. The Lord gives himself to us in bodily form. That is why we must likewise respond to him bodily. That means above all that the Eucharist must reach out beyond the limits of the church itself in the manifold forms of service to men and to the world. But it also means that our religion, our prayer, demands bodily expression. Because the Lord, the Risen One, gives himself in the Body, we have to respond in soul and body. All the spiritual possibilities of our body are necessarily included in celebrating the Eucharist: singing, speaking, keeping silence, sitting, standing, kneeling. Perhaps in the past we too much neglected singing and speaking and simply kept silence side by side; today, on the contrary, we run the risk of forgetting about keeping silence. But only all three together—singing, speaking, keeping

---

[11] I had already tried to expound the same basic idea in the little booklet *Sakramentale Begründung christlicher Existenz* [The sacramental basis of Christian living] (Freising, 1966), pp. 26f. This text, giving a mere outline, was written before the development of the dispute about the Eucharist in the years since the Council and had in the meantime given rise to the misapprehension that I intended thereby to deny the Real Presence and to oppose adoration. I hope that the exposition given here will leave no room for this misunderstanding.

silence—constitute the response in which the full capacity of our spiritual body opens up for the Lord. The same is true of the three bodily attitudes: sitting, standing, kneeling. Again, perhaps in the past we too far forgot standing and, to some extent, sitting, as an expression of relaxed listening and practiced kneeling too exclusively; there, too, we find ourselves today running the opposite risk. And yet here, too, we need the particular mode of expression of all three. Sitting to concentrate on listening to the word of God is part of the Liturgy. Standing, as a sign of readiness, is part of it, just as Israel ate the paschal lamb standing to manifest its readiness to depart and be led by the word of God. Besides that, standing is the expression of the victory of Christ: At the end of a duel it is the victor who is standing. That is what it means when Stephen, before his martyrdom, sees Christ standing at the right hand of God (Acts 7:56). Thus our standing for the Gospel is, over and beyond the Exodus attitude, which we share with Israel, standing in the presence of the Risen One, a recognition of victory.

Finally, kneeling is also essential: as the bodily expression of adoration, in which we remain upright, ready, available, but at the same time bow before the greatness of the living God and of his Name. Jesus Christ himself, according to Saint Luke's account, in the last hours before his Passion, prayed on his knees on the Mount of Olives (Lk 22:41). Stephen fell on his knees when just before his martyrdom he saw the heavens open and Christ standing there (Acts 7:60). Before him who was standing, he knelt. Peter prayed kneeling to beseech God to raise up Tabitha (Acts 9:40). After his great farewell speech before the elders of Ephesus (before he went off to Jerusalem and to his captivity), Paul knelt and prayed with them (Acts 20:36). The most profound teaching is in the hymn to Christ in the Letter to the Philippians (Phil

2:6–11), which refers the promise in Isaiah, of people paying homage on their knees to the God of Israel, to Jesus Christ: He is the "name, that at the name . . . every knee should bow, in heaven and on earth and under the earth" (Phil 2:10). From this text we learn, not only the fact that the primitive Church knelt down before Jesus, but also her reason: She thereby rendered homage to him—to the Crucified One— publicly, as the ruler of the world, in whom the promise of the worldwide rule of the God of Israel has been fulfilled. She thereby gave witness to her faith, over against the Jews, that the law and the prophets are speaking about Jesus when they mention the "Name" of God; as against the Caesar worship—the totalitarian claims of politics—she insisted on the new worldwide dominion of Jesus, which sets limits to political power. She expressed her affirmation of the divinity of Jesus. We kneel with Jesus; we kneel with his witnesses— from Stephen, Peter, and Paul onward—before Jesus, and this is an expression of faith, which was from the beginning the requisite visible witness of the relationship of faith to God and to Christ in this world. Kneeling in this way is the bodily expression of our positive response to the real presence of Jesus Christ, who as God and man, with body and soul, flesh and blood is present among us.

"What great nation is there, that has a god so near to it as the Lord our God is to us?" Let us beseech the Lord to reawaken in us the joy at his presence and that we may once more adore him. Without adoration, there is no transformation of the world.

The Immediacy of
the Presence of the Lord
Carried into Everyday Life

*On the Question of the Adoration of the Eucharist
and Its Sacredness*

The Liturgy for this evening before Maundy Thursday includes the consecration of holy oil for baptism, confirmation,
the ordination of priests, and the anointing of the sick. All
these sacraments, whenever they are celebrated in our diocese, thus stem from what happens in this paschal moment.
It should thus be clear to us that all sacramental acts have
their origin in the Paschal Mystery of the Lord's Cross and
Resurrection. At the same time, however, the sacraments are
thereby united in this one place, our cathedral church, and set
with this church in the unity of the Catholic Church, the
unity of all bishops, in the unity of that chain of laying-on of
hands which takes us back to the calling of the first apostles,
to that hour by the Lake of Genesareth, to the Last Supper
and that time after the Resurrection of the Lord. We are all
anointed at baptism and confirmation. So today we are
going to try to enter likewise from within into the great unity
of the Body of Christ, into the Paschal Mystery from which
our healing comes; to ask the Lord that we may live out
ever more truly our baptism and confirmation and may thus
become worthy also of his eucharistic presence.

The Chrism Mass that we are celebrating today gives particular emphasis, from amid the Paschal Mystery as a whole, to the mission of a priest, which like all sacraments has its origin and its continuing basis in the Cross and Resurrection of Jesus Christ. Again this year the Holy Father has sent a letter to all priests to help us understand our task anew in the light of the Paschal Mystery and, thus, in unity with the whole Church, to live it more fully.[1] On that account we make our recollection this day in fellowship with all the faithful, because our service is to them: even when we are talking about the priesthood, precisely then we are not proclaiming ourselves but Christ crucified, in whose service we are here.

In his letter the Holy Father has turned this year to questions concerning the eucharistic sacrament and has quite deliberately addressed those points on which we risk becoming in some sense one-sided. It is a matter, as people would say nowadays, of a sort of "révision de vie", an examination of our common path at a certain point, so as to find our course again and clarify it. This evening I would like to take two main points out of the Pope's letter and reflect on them with you before the Lord: the question of the adoration of the most holy Eucharist, and that of its sacredness.

First, there is *eucharistic adoration*. We had rediscovered with renewed clarity in the Council that the heart of the eucharistic sacrament is the celebration of the holy mystery in which the Lord assembles his people, unites them, and builds them up by taking them into his sacrifice and giving himself to them, letting himself be received by us. The Eucharist, as we had rediscovered, is an assembly in which the Lord acts

[1] Letter *Dominicae Cenae*, subtitled "The Eucharistic Mystery in the Life of the Church and of the Priest" (1980).

upon us and brings us together. All this is correct and remains correct. But in the meantime this idea of assembly had become flattened and separated from the idea of sacrifice, and thus the Eucharist had shrunk to a mere sign of brotherly fellowship. At the same time the concentration on the eucharistic celebration was causing faith and sacrament to lose something of their place among us. This has become quite visible in many churches—the place of adoration hides away somewhere on the edge of things, like a bit of the past. What was more far-reaching was the way the Eucharist itself was shrinking to the space of a brief half-hour, so that it could no longer breathe life into the building, no longer be the pulse of time. Confined to the space of the sacred rite, it was becoming a tiny island of time on the edge of the day, which as a whole was given over to the profane and hectic business of our worldly activity. If, today, we look back on this development, we realize that the adoration of the sacrament was not in competition with the living celebration of the community, but its condition, its indispensable environment. Only within the breathing space of adoration can the eucharistic celebration indeed be alive; only if the church and thus the whole congregation is constantly imbued with the waiting presence of the Lord, and with our silent readiness to respond, can the invitation to come together bring us into the hospitality of Jesus Christ and of the Church, which is the precondition of the invitation.

The Pope has further clarified these interconnections with a series of reflections. A first of these has been touched on in what was just said: Eucharistic adoration is, as it were, the vertical dimension in which universal and special priesthood coincide. If the distinction of the two callings over against each other is expressed in the Mass, in adoration we see how they are joined together: of this sacrament we all receive. All of us can only stand before him and adore. Even the authority of the priest must in the end be adoration, must spring from adoration and culminate in adoration. And thereby something else becomes clear: Communion and adoration do not stand side by side, or even in opposition, but are indivisibly one. For communicating means entering into fellowship. Communicating with Christ means having fellowship with him. That is why Communion and contemplation belong together: a person cannot communicate with another person without knowing him. He must be open for him, see him, and hear him. Love or friendship always carries within it an impulse of reverence, of adoration. Communicating with Christ therefore demands that we gaze on him, allow him to gaze on us, listen to him, get to know him. Adoration is simply the personal aspect of Communion.

We cannot communicate sacramentally without doing it personally. Sacramental Communion becomes empty, and finally a judgment for us, unless it is repeatedly completed by us personally. The saying of the Lord in the book of Revelation is valid not only for the end times: "Behold, I stand at the door and knock; if any one hears my voice and opens the door, I will come in to him and eat with him, and he with me" (3:20). This is at the same time a description of the most profound content of eucharistic piety. True Communion can happen only if we hear the voice of the Lord, if we answer and open the door. Then he will enter in with us and eat with us. Because this is so, I would like to underline and emphasize two thoughts in the papal letter: "Let us be generous with our time in going to meet him in adoration and . . . [let] our adoration never cease." [2] And the other is connected with this: the Pope heavily emphasizes the intimate

---

[2] Ibid., no. 3, last paragraph.

personal relationship with Christ as the heart of eucharistic piety.[3] In the death of Jesus Christ, says the Pope, each one of us has been loved to the end.[4] Too narrow a conception of the humanity of Jesus Christ has meanwhile sometimes prevented our being aware of this: The Lord knows me, too, and did know me; he suffered for me as well.

And a further aspect expounded in the papal letter is connected with this: The adoration of the Lord in the sacrament is also an education in sensitizing our conscience. "Christ comes into the hearts of our brothers and sisters and visits their consciences."[5] When the conscience becomes dulled, this lets in the violence that lays waste the world. Anyone who gazes upon the face of the Lord, which the servants of the Sanhedrin and Pilate's servants have spat upon, which they have slapped and covered with spittle, will see in his face the mirror of our violence, a reflection of what sin is, and their conscience will be purified in the way that is the precondition for every social reform, for every improvement in human affairs. For the reform of human relationships rests in the first place on a reinforcement of moral strength. Only morality can set limits to violence and selfishness, and wherever it becomes insignificant it is man who is the loser every time, and the weak first of all.

Thus the Pope also tells us that eucharistic adoration "is an education in active love of one's neighbor".[6] It is not just God whom we venerate in eucharistic adoration: "Eucharistic worship is not so much worship of the inaccessible transcendence as worship of the divine condescension."[7] Jesus Christ's sacrifice of his life meets us here and, within this, love

[3] Ibid., no. 4, second paragraph.
[4] Ibid., no. 3, third paragraph.
[5] Ibid., no. 6, second paragraph.
[6] Ibid., first paragraph.
[7] Ibid., no. 7, last paragraph but one.

itself. But we can only understand love by sharing in it, by loving. "Let all pastoral activity be nourished by it, and may it also be food for ourselves and for all the priests who collaborate with us and, likewise, for the whole of the communities entrusted to us. In this practice there should thus be revealed, almost at every step, that close relationship between the Church's spiritual and apostolic vitality and the Eucharist, understood in its profound significance and from all points of view." [8]

Let us now turn to the second aspect, the *sacred nature* of the Eucharist. Our thinking over the last fifteen years has been influenced rather by the notion of "desacralization". We had been struck by the saying in the Letter to the Hebrews that Christ suffered outside the gate (13:12). This, again, chimed in with the other saying, that at the death of the Lord the veil of the Temple was torn in two. Now the Temple is empty. The true holiness, the holy presence of God, is no longer dwelling there; it is outside the city gate. The cult has been transposed out of the holy building into the life, suffering, and death of Jesus Christ. That is where its true presence was already, in his lifetime. When the Temple veil was torn across, so we had thought, the boundary between sacred and profane was torn apart. The cult is no longer something set apart from ordinary life, but holiness dwells in everyday things. What is holy is no longer a special, separate sphere but has chosen to be everywhere, has chosen to make itself felt even in worldly things. Entirely practical conclusions have been drawn from this, right down to some concerning priestly dress, concerning Christian worship and church buildings. This razing of the bastions should be carried out everywhere; nowhere

---

[8] Ibid., no. 4, last paragraph.

should cult and life be any longer distinguishable one from the other. But thereby the message of the New Testament had ultimately been subject to substantial misunderstanding, albeit on the basis of an idea that was itself correct. For God is not withdrawing from the world so as to leave it to its worldliness, any more than he is affirming it in its worldliness, as if this were in itself holy. For as long as the world is imperfect, the distinction within it between sacred and profane will remain, for God is not withdrawing from it the presence of his holiness, and yet his holiness still does not comprehend the whole.

The suffering of Jesus outside the city wall and the tearing in two of the Temple veil does not mean that the Temple is now either everywhere or nowhere at all. That will not be the case until the New Jerusalem. Rather, these things mean that with the death of Jesus Christ the wall between Israel and the world of the nations has been broken down. They mean that God's promise has stepped out of the narrow framework of the Old Covenant and its Temple into the wide world of the nations. They mean that the place of the merely symbolic holiness of the Old Testament images has been taken by the true holiness, the holy Lord in his love become man. Finally, they mean that henceforth the holy tent of God and the cloud of his presence are found wherever the mystery of his Body and Blood is celebrated, wherever men leave off their own activity to enter into fellowship with him. That means that the holiness is more concentrated and powerful than it used to be in the Old Covenant, because it is more true; it also means that that has become more vulnerable and demands of us still greater respect and reverence: not only ritual purity, but the comprehensive preparation of the heart. It demands that we lead lives directed toward the New Jerusalem, that we bring the world into the presence of Jesus Christ, and that we purify it for this; that we take the presence of Jesus Christ into everyday life and thereby transform it. Reverence has become, not superfluous, but more demanding. And because man is made up of body and soul and is, further, a social animal, that is why, now and for the future, we need a visible expression of reverence, the rules of play for its social form, for its visible sign in this sick and unholy world. People are not shaped merely from within outward; another line of influence runs from without inward, and to overlook this or to deny its existence is a kind of spiritualism that soon takes its toll. Holiness, the Holy One, is there in this world, and whenever the educative effect of his visible expression disappears, this leads both people and the world to become more superficial and more barbarous.

In his letter to priests the Holy Father reminds us of a particularly striking sign of reverence in the Roman Liturgy: the hands of the priest are anointed. There is perhaps no organ as much as the hand that so clearly shows the special place of man in the world: parted from the ground, it shows how man walks upright. We give and we take with our hands; we heal and we hit with our hands. Among all peoples, men lift up their hands whenever they turn in prayer to him who is above them. Our hands are anointed. Our hands are bound in duty to the Lord. We are allowed to touch him. What a holy obligation for our whole will and being, what a change it might bring, and would necessarily bring, if we felt the demands made upon us and the direction given us by this sign, day after day. Let us ask the Lord that this sign of the anointing of our hands may more and more be made real in our lives, that our hands may more and more be instruments of blessing, that through his mercy we ourselves may become a blessing and, thus, receive blessing.

The Lord Is Near Us
in Our Conscience,
in His Word,
in His Personal Presence
in the Eucharist

A Homily on Deuteronomy 4:7

In today's reading there is a marvelous saying, in which we can sense all the joy of Israel at its redemption: "What great nation is there that has a god so near to it as the LORD our God is to us, whenever we call upon him?" (Deut 4:7).

Saint Thomas Aquinas took up this saying in his reflections for the Feast of Corpus Christi.[1] In doing so, he showed how we Christians in the Church of the New Covenant can pronounce these words with yet more reason and more joy and with thankfulness than Israel could; in doing so, he showed how this saying, in the Church of Jesus Christ, has acquired a depth of meaning hitherto unsuspected: God has truly come to dwell among us in the Eucharist. He became flesh so that he might become bread. He gave himself to enter into the "fruit of the earth and the work of human hands"; thus he puts himself in our hands and into our hearts. God is not the great unknown, whom we can but

---

[1] Thomas Aquinas, *Officium de festo Corporis Christi*, in *Sanctae Thomae Aquinatis*, ed. R. Busa, S.J. (Stuttgart and Bad Canstatt, 1980), 6:581 = DSG ps. 3, n. 3; ps. 5, n. 3.

dimly conceive. We need not fear, as heathen do, that he might be capricious and bloodthirsty or too far away and too great to hear men. He is there, and we always know where we can find him, where he allows himself to be found and is waiting for us. Today this should once more sink into our hearts: God is near. God knows us. God is waiting for us in Jesus Christ in the Blessed Sacrament. Let us not leave him waiting in vain! Let us not, through distraction and lethargy, pass by the greatest and most important thing life offers us. We should let ourselves be reminded, by today's reading, of the wonderful mystery kept close within the walls of our churches. Let us not pass it heedlessly by. Let us take time, in the course of the week, in passing, to go in and spend a moment with the Lord who is so near. During the day our churches should not be allowed to be dead houses, standing empty and seemingly useless. Jesus Christ's invitation is always being proffered from them. This sacred proximity to us is always alive in them. It is always calling us and inviting us in. This is what is lovely about Catholic churches, that within them there is, as it were, always worship, because the eucharistic presence of the Lord dwells always within them.

And a second thing: let us never forget that Sunday is the Lord's day. It is not an arbitrary decision of the Church, requiring us to attend Mass on Sunday. This is never a duty laid upon us from without; it is the royal privilege of the Christian to share in paschal fellowship with the Lord, in the Paschal Mystery. The Lord has made the first day of the week his own day, on which he comes to us, on which he spreads the table for us and invites us to share with him. We can see, in the Old Testament passage at which we are looking, that the Israelites saw in the presence of God, not a burden, but the basis of their pride and their joy. And indeed the Sunday fellowship with the Lord is not a burden, but a grace, a gift, which lights up the whole week, and we would be cheating ourselves if we withdrew from it.

"What great nation is there that has a god so near to it as the LORD our God is to us, whenever we call upon him?" This passage from the Old Testament has found its ultimate depth of meaning in the eucharistic presence of the Lord. But its earlier meaning is not thereby abolished, but merely purified and exalted. We must now investigate that, in order to understand what the Lord is saying to us here. In the chapter of the book of Deuteronomy from which this passage is taken, the marvelous closeness of God is seen above all in the law he has given to Israel through Moses. Through the law he makes himself permanently available, as it were, for the questions of his people. Through the law he can always be spoken with by Israel; she can call on him, and he answers. Through the law he offers Israel the opportunity to build a social and political order that breaks new ground. Through the law he makes Israel wise and shows her the way a man should live, so as to live aright. In the law Israel experiences the close presence of God; he has, as it were, drawn back the veil from the riddles of human life and replied to the obscure questionings of men of all ages: Where do we come from? Where are we going? What must we do?

This joy in the law astounds us. We have become used to regarding it as a burden that oppresses man. At its best periods, Israel saw in the law in fact something that set them free for the truth, free from the burden of uncertainty, the gracious gift of the way. And, indeed, we do know today that man collapses if he has constantly to reinvent himself, if he has to create anew human existence. For man, the will of God is not a foreign force of exterior origin, but the actual orientation of his own being. Thus the revelation of God's will is the revelation of what our own being truly wishes—it is a gift. So we should learn anew to be grateful that in the word of God the will of God and the meaning of our own existence have been communicated to us. God's presence in the word and his presence in the Eucharist belong together, inseparably. The eucharistic Lord is himself the living Word. Only if we are living in the sphere of God's Word can we properly comprehend and properly receive the gift of the Eucharist.

Today's Gospel reading[2] makes us aware, besides this, of a third aspect. The law became a burden the moment it was no longer being lived out from within but was broken down into a series of obligations external in their origin and their nature. Thus the Lord tells us emphatically: The true law of God is not an external matter. It dwells within us. It is the inner direction of our lives, which is brought into being and established by the will of God. It speaks to us in our conscience. The conscience is the inner aspect of the Lord's presence, which alone can render us capable of receiving the eucharistic presence. That is why that same book of Deuteronomy, from which our reading today was taken, says elsewhere: "The word is very near you; it is in your mouth and in your heart, so that you can do it" (Deut 30:14; cf. Rom 10:8). Faith in Christ simply renders the inmost part of our being, our conscience, once more articulate. The Holy Father, John Paul II, says on this point: "In a person's obedience to his conscience lies both the key to his moral stature and the basis of his 'royal dignity'. . . . Obedience to one's conscience is . . . the Christian's participation in the 'royal priesthood' of Christ. Obedience to the conscience . . . makes 'to serve . . . Christ' actually mean 'to reign'." [3]

---

[2] Gospel for the 22nd Sunday in Ordinary Time, Year B: Mark 7:1–8, 14–15, 21–23.

[3] John Paul II, *Zeichen des Widerspruchs: Besinnung auf Christus* (Zürich, 1979), pp. 162f.

The Lord is near us in our conscience, in his word, in his personal presence in the Eucharist: this constitutes the dignity of the Christian and is the reason for his joy. We rejoice therefore, and this joy is expressed in praising God. Today we can see how the closeness of the Lord also brings people together and brings them close to each other: it is because we have the same Lord Jesus Christ in Munich and in Rome that we form one single people of God, across all frontiers, united in the call of conscience, united by the word of God, united through communion with Jesus Christ, united in the praise of God, who is our joy and our redemption.

Standing before the Lord— Walking with the Lord— Kneeling before the Lord

Celebrating Corpus Christi

If we want to understand the meaning of Corpus Christi, the best thing to do is simply to look at the liturgical form in which the Church celebrates and expounds the significance of this feast. Over and above the elements common to all Christian feasts, there are three components especially that constitute the distinctive shape of the way we celebrate this day.

First there is what we are doing right now, meeting together around the Lord, *standing before the Lord*, for the Lord, and thus standing side by side together. Next there is *walking with the Lord*, the procession. And finally there is the heart and the climax of it, *kneeling before the Lord*, the adoration, glorifying him and rejoicing in his presence. Standing before the Lord, walking with the Lord, and kneeling before the Lord, these three therefore are the constituent elements of this day, and we are now going to reflect on them a little.

One Body

Standing before the Lord: In the early Church there was an expression for this: *statio*. And when I mention that term, we touch on the oldest roots of what happens on Corpus Christi and what Corpus Christi is about. At the time when Christianity was spreading out across the world, from the beginning its representatives laid great emphasis on having in each city just one bishop, only one altar. This was supposed to express the unity brought by the one Lord, who embraces us in his arms outstretched on the Cross, transcending all the barriers and limits traced by earthly life, and makes us one Body. And this is the inmost meaning of the Eucharist, that we, receiving the *one* bread, enter into this *one* heart and thus become a living organism, the *one* Body of the Lord.

The Eucharist is not a private business, carried on in a circle of friends, in a club of like-minded people, who seek out and get together with those who already suit them; but just as the Lord allowed himself to be crucified outside the city wall, before all the world, and stretches out his hands to everyone, thus the Eucharist is the public worship of all those whom the Lord calls, irrespective of their personal make-up. It is particularly characteristic of him, as he demonstrated in his earthly life, to have men of the most diverse groupings, social backgrounds, and personal views brought together in the greater whole of his word and his love. It was characteristic of the Eucharist, then, in the Mediterranean world in which Christianity first developed, for an aristocrat who had found his way into Christianity to sit there side by side with a Corinthian dock worker, a miserable slave, who under Roman law was not even regarded as a man but was treated as chattel. It was characteristic of the Eucharist for the philosopher to sit next to the illiterate man, the converted prostitute and the converted tax collector next to the religious ascetic who had found his way to Jesus Christ. And we can see in the writings of the New Testament how people resisted this again and again, wanted to stay in their own circle, and yet this very thing remained the point of the Eucharist: gathering together, crossing the boundaries, and leading men through the Lord into a new unity.

When Christianity grew in numbers, this exterior form could no longer be maintained in the cities. As early as the time of persecutions, the titular churches in Rome, for instance, were already developing as precursors of the later parishes. Even here, of course, the public nature and the given structure of worship remained, so that people who would otherwise never meet were brought together. But this opening up of relationships within a single space was no longer sufficiently visible. That is why they developed the custom of the *statio*. That means that the pope, as the one bishop of Rome, especially in the course of Lent, leads the worship for the whole of Rome and goes right through each of the titular churches. The Christians meet together, go to the church together, and thus in each particular church the whole becomes visible and touches each individual. This basic idea is taken up by Corpus Christi. It is a *statio urbis*: we open up the parish churches; we open up for ourselves all the odd corners and farthest reaches of this city to be brought together to the Lord, so as to be at one through him. Here, too, we are together irrespective of party or class, rulers and ruled, men who work with their hands and those who do mental work, men of this tendency or that. And this is the essential thing, that we have been brought together by the Lord, that he leads us to meet each other. This moment should issue a call to us to accept one another inwardly, open ourselves up, go to meet each other, that even in the distraction of everyday life we should maintain this state of being brought together by the Lord.

Our cities, as we all know, have become places of solitude of a kind never known before. And nowhere are people so lonely and abandoned as perhaps in apartment complexes, where they are packed together most closely. A friend told me how once, when he had moved into a big city in the north, he was on his way out of the apartment complex, and he greeted someone else who lived in that complex, but the person just stared at him in amazement and said, "You've mistaken me for someone else!" Where people are just masses, a greeting turns into a mistake. But the Lord brings us together and opens us up, so that we can accept one another, belong to one another, so that in standing before him we can learn again to stand next to each other. Thus, the Marienplatz itself comes into its own true rôle. How often we hurry past each other here. Today this is the setting for our being together, which, as a duty and a gift, will continue. There are of course many big gatherings, yet so often it is what we are against that unites us, more than what we are for. And it is almost always the case that we are brought together by something we want, and this interest is directed against other such interests. But what unites us today is not the private interest of this group or that, but the interest that God takes in us, to which we can calmly confide all our own interests and wishes. We are standing for the Lord. And the more we stand for the Lord and before the Lord, the more we stand with one another, and our capacity to understand one another grows again, the capacity to recognize each other as people, as brothers and sisters, and thus, in being together, to build the basis and to open up the possibilities of humanity and of life.

Standing together in the Lord's presence, and with the Lord, has resulted from the beginning in what it has indeed at its heart presupposed, *walking to the Lord*. For we are not automatically side by side. That is why a *statio* could happen only if people gathered beforehand and went to each other in the *processio*. That is the second call issued by Corpus Christi. We can stand side by side only if, first of all, under the guidance of the Lord, we go to each other. We can come to the Lord only in this *procedere*, in this moving out and moving forward, by transcending our own prejudices, our limits, and our barriers, going forward, going toward him, and moving to the point at which we can meet each other. This also is as true in the realm of the Church as in the world. Even in the Church—let us lament before God—there are conflict, opposition, and mistrust. *Processio, procedere*, should challenge us to move forward again, to go ahead toward him, and to subject ourselves to his measure and in our common belief in him who became man, who gives himself to us as bread, once more trusting each other, opening up to each other, and together letting ourselves be led by him.

The procession, which from an early period was a part of the stational worship in Rome, certainly did acquire a new dimension, a new depth, in Corpus Christi. For the Corpus Christi procession is no longer just walking to the Lord, to the eucharistic celebration; it is walking with the Lord; it is itself an element of eucharistic celebration, one dimension of the eucharistic event. The Lord who has become our bread is thus showing us the way, is in fact our way, as he leads us. In this fashion the Church offered a new interpretation of the Exodus story, of Israel's wandering in the wilderness, about which we heard in the reading. Israel travels through the wilderness. And it is able to find a path in the pathless wilderness, because the Lord is leading it in the guise of cloud and of light. It can live in the pathless and lifeless wilderness because man does not live by bread alone but by every word that proceeds from the mouth of God. And so in this story of Israel's journey through the wilderness the underlying meaning of all human history is revealed. This Israel was able to find a country and was able to survive after the loss of that country because it did not live from bread alone, but found in the Word the strength to live on through all the pathless and homeless wilderness of the centuries. And this is thus an enduring sign set up for us all. Man finds his way only if he will let himself be led by him who is Word and bread in one.

Only in walking with the Lord can we endure the peregrinations of our history. Thus Corpus Christi expounds the meaning of our whole life, of the whole history of the world: marching toward the promised land, a march that can keep on in the right direction only if we are walking with him who came among us as bread and Word. Today we know better than earlier ages that indeed the whole life of this world and the history of mankind is in movement, an incessant transformation, and moving onward. The word *progress* has acquired an almost magical ring. Yet we know, at the same time, that progress can be a meaningful term only if we know where we want to go. Mere movement in itself is not progress. It can just as well represent a rapid descent into the abyss. So if there is to be progress, we must ask how to measure it and what we are aiming at, certainly not merely an increase in material production. Corpus Christi expounds the meaning of history. It offers the measure, for our wandering through this world, of Jesus Christ, who became man, the eucharistic Lord who shows us the way. Not every problem, of course, is solved thereby. That just is not the way God goes about things. He gives us our freedom and our capacities so that we can make efforts, discover things, and struggle with things. But the basic yardstick has been laid down. And whenever we look to him as the measure and the goal of our path, then a criterion has been given that makes it possible to distinguish the right path from the wrong: walking with the Lord, as the sign and as the duty of this day.

And finally there is *kneeling before the Lord*: adoration. Because he himself is present in the Eucharist, adoration has always been an essential part of it. Even if it was not developed in this form of a great feast until the Middle Ages, nonetheless it is not a change or a form of decadence; it is nothing essentially different, but merely the complete emergence of what was already there. For if the Lord gives himself to us, then receiving him can only mean to bow before him, to glorify him, to adore him. And even today it is not contrary to the dignity and freedom and status of man to bow his knee, to be obedient to him, to worship him and glorify him. For if we deny him, so as not to have to adore him, then what remains is merely the eternal necessity of physical material. Then we are truly bereft of freedom, a mere speck of dust that is flung around among the mill wheels of the universe and that vainly tries to persuade itself of having freedom. Only if he is the Creator is freedom the basis of all things; only then can we be free. And when our freedom bows before him, it is not abrogated but is at that moment truly accepted and rendered definitive.

But today there is one additional thing. The One whom we adore—as I was saying—is not some distant power. He has himself knelt down before us to wash our feet. And that gives to our adoration the quality of being unforced, adoration in joy and in hope, because we are bowing down before him who himself bowed down, because we bow down to enter into a love that does not make slaves of us but transforms us. So let us ask the Lord that he may grant us to understand this and to rejoice in it and that this understanding and this joy may spread out from this day far and wide into our country and our everyday life.

We Who Are Many Are One Body, One Bread (1 Corinthians 10:17)

The Eucharist and the Church

Augustine briefly sums up his explanation of what the Eucharist is, which he has given in a sermon for those newly baptized at the Easter Vigil,[1] in the following words: "It needs to be made clear to you what it is that you have received. Hear briefly, then, what the apostle—or, rather, Christ through the apostle—says about the sacrament of the Body of the Lord. 'We who are many are one Body, . . . one Bread' (1 Cor 10:17). Behold, that is all; I have told it to you quickly; but weigh these words, do not count them!"

In his view, there is, in this one sentence of the apostle, the whole mystery of what they are receiving. There are not many words, but they are weighty words. The main emphasis of the Eucharist here becomes apparent: the Eucharist is instrumental in the process by which Christ builds himself a Body and makes us into one single Bread, one single Body. The content of the Eucharist, what happens in it, is the uniting of Christians, bringing them from their state of separation into the unity of the one Bread and the one Body. The

[1] *Tractatus de dominica sanctae Paschae*, ed. G. Morin, *Miscellanea Agostiniana*, vol. 1 (Rome, 1930), pp. 462–64.

Eucharist is thus understood entirely in a dynamic ecclesi-ological perspective. It is the living process through which, time and again, the Church's activity of becoming the Church takes place.

The Church is eucharistic fellowship. She is not just a people: out of the many peoples of which she consists there is arising *one* people, through the *one* table that the Lord has spread for us all. The Church is, so to speak, a network of eucharistic fellowships, and she is united, ever and again, through the *one* Body we all receive.

Peace from the Lord

"Peace" as One of the Names of the Eucharistic Sacrament

Grace and peace from God, our Father, and from Christ. This is the task of the priest and the bishop: to call into our age, again and again, the grace and peace of the Lord. This is in the first instance a quite human appeal, that we should be men of grace and of peace in our dealings with one another, that we should not be forever keeping account, that we should be capable of drawing a line under things, not thinking about unsettled accounts, not people who allow the poison of resentment to fester and spread within them, but who are capable of getting over things, of making a new start. The Greek word for "grace", *charis*, derives from the word for "joy" and means at the same time rejoicing, joy, and also beauty, pleasure, sympathy. Where all this is present—just for once setting aside what we could perhaps still demand; beginning again; generosity of the heart, which does not keep something stored up in some corner of our memory for bringing out later—there joy can grow, there beauty springs up, there goodness shines out into the world, and peace comes to be.

Certainly, these human actions of ours and our human will are never in the end enough. And the priest is never merely a preacher of morality. He proclaims something we humans cannot give: the new reality that comes to us from God, in

Christ, and that is more than just words and intentions. The early Church understood the mystery of the Eucharist as underlying the expression *"peace"*. "Peace" very quickly became one of the names for the eucharistic sacrament, for it is there that God does in fact come to meet us, that he sets us free, that, although we are debtors, guilty in his sight, he takes us in his arms, gives himself to us. And by leading us to himself, introducing us into the communion of his Body, by introducing us into the same sphere of his love, by feeding us with the same Bread, he also gives us to one another as brothers and sisters. The Eucharist is peace from the Lord.

The Christian Faith as a Peace Movement

At the beginning of Christian history the faithful were a marginal group, politically insignificant. They themselves were unable actively to participate in the shaping of public policy on any matter. Nonetheless, the peace of Christ was for them not merely an inner peace and not merely a future peace. The first words of the Risen One to his confused disciples had been: Peace be with you (Jn 20:19). In each eucharistic assembly what happened on the evening of Easter Day was repeated for them. The Risen One came in among his disciples and spoke to them: Peace be with you. In this their paschal feast, in which the Church was truly alive, they experienced how the apostle's saying is true: Christ is our peace (Eph 2:14). Here they met with the new sphere of peace that faith had opened up—the reconciliation of slaves and free men, of Greeks and barbarians, of Jews and gentiles (cf. Gal 3:28). Here, they who were deeply divided one from another in the framework of the society of that time were at one, were indeed one single person—the new man, Jesus

Christ, who on the basis of the Father's love bound them all together (cf. Gal 3:17, 28). That is why the Eucharist itself was often simply referred to as "peace": it was the place of the presence of Jesus Christ and was thereby the sphere of a new peace, the sphere of a table fellowship that transcended all boundaries and limits, in which everyone was at home everywhere. The bishops of the whole world notified their election to each other by letters of peace. Any carrier of a letter of peace who came upon Christians somewhere was among his own family, wherever it was, a brother among brethren. It was with the inmost element of their faith, with the eucharistic assembly, that the early Christians thus did something politically most significant: they created spheres of peace and built, as it were, highroads of peace through a world of strife.[1]

[1] Cf. on this point H. de Lubac, *Quellen christlicher Einheit* (Einsiedeln, 1974); L. Bouyer, *Die Kirche*, vol. 1 (Einsiedeln, 1977), pp. 19–37; L. Hertling, "Communio und Primat", *Una Sancta* 17 (1962): 91–125.

A Church of All Times
and Places

Celebrating in Communion with the Pope

In the fundamental prayer of the Church, the Eucharist, the
heart of our life is not merely expressed but is realized day
after day. At the most profound level, the Eucharist has to do
with Christ alone. He prays for us; he puts his prayer on our
lips, for only he can say: This is my Body—This is my Blood.
Thus he draws us into his life, into the act of eternal love by
which he gives himself up to the Father, so that we are made
over into the Father's possession with him and that through
this very act Jesus Christ himself is bestowed upon us. Thus
the Eucharist is *a sacrifice*: being given up to God in Jesus
Christ and thereby at the same time having the gift of his love
bestowed on us, for Christ is both the giver and gift. Through
him, and with him, and in him we celebrate the Eucharist. In
the Eucharist, what the epistle for today says is constantly
present and real: Christ is the head of the Church, which he
wins evermore with his blood.

At the same time, at every celebration of the Eucharist we
say, in accordance with ancient tradition: We celebrate together with our pope. . . . Christ gives himself in the Eucharist, and he is entirely present in each place, so that wherever
the Eucharist is celebrated, the whole mystery of the Church

is present. But in all places, Christ is only one, and on that account we cannot receive him against others or without others. Precisely because it is the whole Christ, the undivided and indivisible Christ, who gives himself in the Eucharist, for that very reason the Eucharist can be celebrated rightly only if it is celebrated with the whole Church. We have Christ only if we have him together with others. Because the Eucharist is concerned only with Christ, it is a sacrament of the Church. And for the same reason it can be carried on only in unity with the whole Church and with her authority. That is why the pope belongs in the Eucharistic Prayer, in the eucharistic celebration. Communion with him is that communion with the whole, without which there is no communion with Christ. A part of Christian prayer and of the Christian act of faith is committing oneself in faith to the whole, overcoming one's own limits. The Liturgy is not the setting up of some club, an association of friends; we receive it from the whole Church, and we have to celebrate it as coming from the whole and directed toward the whole. Only then do we believe and pray aright, when we are living it in the context of this act of self-transcendence, of self-abnegation, directed toward the Church of all times and of all places: this is what Catholicism essentially is. That is what we aim at whenever we step out of the zone of what is ours to unite ourselves with the pope and thus enter into the Church of all nations.

The Church Subsists as Liturgy and in the Liturgy

A Homily on Acts 2:42

> Lord,
> renew the life of your Church
> with the power of this sacrament.
> May the breaking of bread
> and the teaching of the apostles
> keep us united in your love.
> This we ask through Jesus Christ, our Lord.
> —*Prayer after Communion from the Liturgy for*
> *the solemnity of Saints Peter and Paul, Apostles*

The closing prayer from today's Liturgy takes up the picture of the growing Church drawn by Luke in the Acts of the Apostles and turns it into a prayer. It asks that the Church today, and ever anew, may be again the way she was then in her beginning. This corresponds to the original intention of this passage, which was meant to draw an ideal picture of the Church for all time and to say at the same time that the Church springs ever anew from prayer, that she needs ever anew to be asked for in prayer from the Lord.

Now, what is being said here about the Church? It says: "They devoted themselves to the apostles' teaching and fellowship, to the breaking of bread and the prayers" (Acts 2:42). We can see in this a sketch of the primitive Christian service

of worship, which starts with the teaching of the apostles, that
is, with the proclamation and hearing of the faith of the
Church, of the word of God that is alive in her and that thus
becomes the basis for liturgical and living fellowship: it
reaches a climax in the eucharistic encounter with the Lord,
who gives himself to us as bread, and resounds in songs of
praise. The Church is adoration. This passage is telling us that
the Church subsists as *Liturgy* and in Liturgy. She is the living
temple that, even within the stone Temple in Jerusalem, dedicated to destruction, is growing up on the foundation stone
of Christ.

Nonetheless, this does not represent any kind of transfig-
uring or narrowing down, in an aesthetic or liturgical direction, of the situation or the nature of the Church. For the
shape of Christian worship reproduces, at the same time, *both
the way to go and the manner of going in human life.* Human life
is, in the first place, a search for *meaning*, the search for some
message that can show me my path and give me direction.
Because of its whole direction, life is a search for a supportive
community, since man is created for community. It is a search
for a love that shares, that teaches us to trust, and that can be
trusted right to the end in mutual giving. And thus it is a
demand that the world should be transformed by love into
praise: prayer embraces the whole world, and the world is
comprehended within prayer.

Yet it has already become clear that the Church, as a community of adoration and of brotherly service, draws life from
the priestly office, as Cyril of Jerusalem beautifully expressed
it, in the passage where he refers to the fact that the word
ecclesia, church, occurs for the first time in the Bible when
Aaron is invested with the priestly office.[1] Priesthood and

---

[1] Cyril of Jerusalem, *Baptismal Catechesis* 18, par. 24 (PG 33:1046).

the Church come to birth together and belong together indivisibly. To describe the Church is therefore at the same time to explain what is the heart and the meaning of the priestly task: *They devoted themselves to the apostles' teaching and fellowship, to the breaking of bread and the prayers.*

If we look at the sentence rather more closely, we can see the two focal points of the priestly task: service to the Word and service to the sacrament—but in both, the service of God to men and the service of men to God.

First there is *service to the Word*. The priest is entrusted with the task of carrying ever onward before men the lantern of the joyous message of the gospel, so that the words of the psalm may always be true: "Your word is a lamp to my feet." But it is important to see how Luke refers to this word of God that has to be proclaimed in the Church. We would probably expect him to talk about the gospel. But here he does not do so, perhaps because he was already familiar with the way this word was misused, as we see so often today. For wherever anyone refers with emphasis to the gospel over against the Church, God is thereby being appropriated for one's own self; his word is being made someone's private property and often, in the end, a defense against God's will. For it is said that "gospel" means message of joy, and must be that, and consequently can include nothing that I find disagreeable or uncomfortable, still less, challenging or hard.

What is being forgotten here is that in the ancient world this word *evangelium*, gospel, meant the imperial message, which is a message of joy because it comes from the Lord of the world, because whatever comes from the Lord of the world is salvation for the world. As applied to the emperors of ancient time, this was usually mere cynicism. But when it is referred to Jesus Christ, then this expression finds its true meaning: the gospel is the imperial message in which the Lord of the world, the Creator, bows down to us and speaks to us. That the true Lord, the Creator, does not consider himself too great to bow down to us, this alone, that he knows us and is able and willing to accept us, this is a message of salvation; it lifts the fog of questioning, the isolation, the dark loneliness, and lets the light come in. But because this Lord of the world is the Lord of its truth and is love, to the point of dying for men, the message that comes from him is the real good news, good even when it tears us away from the comfort of our narrow middle-class conformism, our self-will, and the way we have settled into our own ideas, so as to lead us out into the great and, at first, painful world of the truth and of real love.

Yet here Luke does not use the word gospel but speaks of their remaining steadfast in the teaching of the apostles. The Lord passed on the word to the apostles, to the Twelve, and thus his word has become an apostolic word, the word of these people who derived their ministry from him only as a community, as the Twelve, and handed it on to us as a community. The apostles represent, on the one hand, the people of God of the future and, on the other, the future structure of this people. And thus it is made clear to us that God's word can never be private property, never my personal possession, but that it lives always in the "we" of the Church, in the people of God built up apostolically. The word does not come to us privately; we receive it through the living tradition of the Church, by sharing her faith and life and that of her living community.

Only when the word is alive in the living community is it protected from decline into a literary or a merely past existence; only then can trustworthiness and dynamism work together; only then can it move on and constantly remain a living word, which is suffered and experienced and is at the same time faithfulness to what we cannot make for ourselves but that is given to us. We receive the word of God from within the apostolic Church, in her faith. Remaining steadfast in the teaching of the apostles, that is your task, dear ordinands: receiving the word from the living Church, keeping it alive, and passing it on. You can do that only if you live together in her, if your life is directed to her true heart, finding in her the earth in which to root your life, and being able then, ever and again, to hand it on to men.

I sometimes have the impression that there is a temptation today to set up beside the pastoral approach of faith, or even against it, a pastoral approach based on one's own cleverness, an approach that no longer actually trusts in faith's ability to call men together today. Because this approach no longer believes that faith can actually affect anything, it has, so to say, to outwit God and men with its cleverness and to build something on its own account. How can that stand the test? It may perhaps seem simpler to begin with. But it remains our own work and still has the weaknesses of what is ours. A bishop from a country with a Marxist government said to me that what was most characteristic of that world, no longer allowed to be open to anything transcendent, was its unbelievable dreariness, the boredom of a world that can expect nothing but itself, the everlasting grayness of leaden everyday life with no celebration, in which, ultimately, nothing else can arrive, because man alone simply reproduces himself. In such a dreary wilderness, in the grayness of merely self-made life, there awakes a longing for something completely different to happen. Vladimir Maximov, the Russian emigré, said, on the basis of a similar experience: For too long already we have talked about man; let us finally talk about God again.

The world needs more than just itself. Amid the dreariness,

people do not need a distraction that will in the end become dreary itself; they are asking for mystery, even if they do not realize this themselves. They need the sign of the wholly other, the living word of God, entering into this our age in unadulterated trustworthiness and dynamism. That is the great task you are taking on at this moment, rooted in the apostolic structure of the Church, to remain steadfast in its word and thus to bring it to fruition: to bring into the world the great and transforming Other, the element without which the world can only sink into gray boredom.

Next to the word stands the *sacrament*. Luke refers to it right away according to what is at its heart: They remained steadfast in the breaking of bread. Ultimately, the Church draws her life from the Eucharist, from this real, self-giving presence of the Lord. Without this ever-new encounter with him, she would necessarily wither. That is why our priesthood, too, draws life from the eucharistic community with the Lord, from the way that the Eucharist is the constant heart and strength of our life. Anyone who repeatedly exposes himself to it and confides in it will be changed. You cannot walk constantly with the Lord, cannot ever anew pronounce these tremendous words, *This is my Body and my Blood*, you cannot touch the Body of the Lord again and again, without being affected by him and challenged by him, being changed and led by him. We may of course lag behind him, and will again and again lag immeasurably far behind, but in the long run there are only really two possibilities: either to shake off the Eucharist, with the enormous demands and power it sets up in life, or to surrender to it, to hold fast to it. Anyone who holds fast to the Lord will not be abandoned by him. Anyone who grapples with him calmly and patiently, humbly and sincerely, will be led by him; he will never be denied his light.

They remained steadfast in the breaking of bread. A parish priest of this diocese, who died this year, once told me, in a most moving way, how he had personally experienced this saying. As a soldier he took part in the invasion of Crete and went to look for a billet in a house. He noticed there how the man who met him was having a struggle because he was suffering on account of this trampling upon his homeland and because he knew that he himself would be in danger if he offered hospitality in this case. But he saw how in the end the man overcame his feelings, invited him to sit at the table, took a piece of bread, broke it in two, and gave him a piece of bread. And he noticed that this was more than a mere gesture; he realized what it meant: I accept you as a guest, as a brother; this is my life, you are protected by my life, just as I accept the danger to myself. He had noticed how, when the man was tearing the bread up, it was as if he were really sharing out his own life, giving of his own without taking notice of the danger threatening him. And still, after nearly forty years, the emotion of this experience, of how that life was shared-out with the bread, still made him tremble.

Christ genuinely shared himself out, gave himself with the torn-up bread, so that his life might be ours: that is the incredible event that occurs ever anew. Herein lies the great significance of the Eucharist, and that is why it is no game, but quite real. When death comes onstage the game is at an end. Man is set before the truth. But only when this encounter reaches right down unto death can true hope arise for man. Christ shares himself with us. Let us take this to heart again and again, so that we may share him out; it is immediately clear that we can devote ourselves to the breaking of bread only if we ourselves become breakers of bread in the fullest sense. Hence the Eucharist is the true motive power for all social transformation in the world. From Elizabeth of Hungary, by way of Nicholas of Flüe and Vincent de Paul, right up to Mother Teresa, it is evident that wherever the gestures of the Lord, the breaker of bread, are accepted, then the breaking of bread must be carried on right into everyday life. There is no longer any stranger there who means nothing to me; rather, there is a brother there who calls on me and who is waiting for the broken bread, to find a resting place in his love.

In his account of the developing Church, Luke also adds: They remained steadfast in *prayer*. That means: They took part in the daily prayer, in Israel's recitation of the Psalms, and that in turn means that in this sense the praying of the breviary is of apostolic origin. The Eucharist, the open gateway to God, and from God to us, cannot be limited to a mere half-hour in the morning. It must find echoes in order to be alive. It must shed light throughout the day. There must be no timetable so watertight, no demarcation so difficult to overcome, as to leave no place for that breathing space of prayer, which serves the health of body and soul and, thereby, the right way of changing this world.

And so I beg you, do not allow this breath of prayer, however pressed you may be, to cease in your everyday priestly life. We need the breath of prayer. You will see how it bears fruit. Let prayer spread its influence in the congregations. In order that the Eucharist may live, they need this space of prayer, which is open to us through the praise of God, rendered possible by praying vespers together. Praying the Rosary and the stations of the Cross, everything by way of prayer that has developed in the fullness of the Christian faith—we need it again today. We need it especially in a world that is bored amid the perfection of its occupations, that is not just preoccupied with itself but wishes to be touched by him who alone can give our lives meaning.

They devoted themselves to the apostles' teaching and fellowship, to the breaking of bread and the prayers. My dear young friends, I ask you to take this passage from today's Liturgy for a motto as you begin your priestly life. Become genuine servants of the Word; live in it, and live in such a fashion as to make it a present reality. Become servants of the Eucharist and of Lord's love, which is preserved in it; and become thereby servants of the joy that will return upon you. But all of us gathered here, who are privileged with you to bear this sacrament, we are praying for you in this hour: that the Lord who has brought you to this point may not leave you, that he may lead you, may fill you through and through with his word and his love, and grant you the fullness of the gospel, the fullness of joy, that comes from the good news.

My Joy Is to Be in Thy Presence

On the Christian Belief in Eternal Life

We look for the resurrection of the dead, and the life of the world to come. That is what we say in the great Creed of the Church, Sunday after Sunday, in the Liturgy. But are we really expecting this resurrection? And eternal life? The statistics tell us that many Christians, even churchgoers, have given up believing in eternal life, or at any rate regard it as a pretty uncertain business. The figures would give even more cause for reflection if we were to get involved in questions like these: Does this expectation play any practical part in our life? Do we find it lovely and consoling to think that we can live eternally, or does that all seem nebulous and unreal, perhaps indeed not even much worth striving for? Hans Urs von Balthasar put the question like this: "It is as if modern man had had a tendon cut, so that he can no longer run toward his original goal, as if his wings had been clipped, as if his spiritual awareness of transcendence had withered. How can that have come about?"[1] Certainly, interest in life after death is not quite so lacking, even today, as at first appears. The desire to see loved ones again is alive today; the

[1] Hans Urs von Balthasar, "Der Mensch und das Ewige Leben" [Man and eternal life], *Internationale katholische Zeitschrift Communio* 20 (1991): 3.

feeling that there might be a judgment and that our life may have to stand that test inevitably occurs to us at the very moment when we are doing something we ourselves recognize to be wrong.

1. Faith in God and the Expectation of Eternal Life

Nonetheless, it is still the case that in modern man, even in today's Christian, the awareness of eternal life has become astoundingly weak; you will rarely get to hear a sermon about heaven, hell, and purgatory today. So let us ask again: How has that come about? I believe it has a great deal to do with our picture of God and of his relation to the world, which from the general consciousness has infiltrated the ideas even of those people who really want to be believers and Christians. We are hardly still able to imagine that God really does anything in the world and with people, that he himself is an active agent in history. That seems to us mythic and unenlightened. The habit of regarding the miracles of the New Testament as not really being that, but as being derived from historically conditioned suppositions, has today become quite normal; even the birth of Jesus from the Virgin and the genuine Resurrection of Jesus, which snatched his body from decay, are at best relegated to the status of insignificant and marginal questions: it seems to make us feel uncomfortable that God should have intervened in biological or physical processes. The world once for all created is closed within itself and its causal relations, even though the picture of reality presented by modern physics no longer offers that ultimate certitude on which people in the last century felt they could rely. What happens in the world can be explained, so we think, only in worldly terms. Apart from ourselves there

God Is Near Us

is no one at work in the world, and that is why we expect nothing from anyone other than ourselves, whom in turn we think we know to be completely dependent upon the laws of nature and of history. God is—as we were saying—no longer an active agent in history but, at best, a hypothesis of marginal status.

The withering of hope in eternity is thus simply the reverse side of the withering of faith in the living God. The belief in eternal life is simply the application to our own existence of faith in God. Hence it can only come to life again if we discover a new relationship with God—if we learn to see God once more as an active agent in the world and in regard to ourselves. "We look for the resurrection of the dead, and the life of the world to come"—this statement is not a further demand for faith, set up beside faith in God; it is simply the unpacking of what it means to believe in God, the Father, the Son, and the Holy Spirit. It is not by analysis of our own existence, not by looking at ourselves, at our hopes and our needs, that we discover eternal life. Eternal life steadily withdraws from a person whose attention is fixed on himself. In turning toward God it becomes obvious that anyone upon whom God has looked, and whom he loves, shares in his eternity. Origen once expressed this insight quite beautifully, saying: "that every being which shares in that eternal nature itself exists forevermore . . . expresses the eternity of the divine loving-kindness." He then adds: "Would it not seem godless to assume that a spirit capable of relating to God should suffer destruction in its substance?" [2]

---

[2] *Peri Archôn* 4, 4:9; *Works*, ed. Koetschau, vol. 5 (GCS 22), p. 362 ; PG 11, col. 413; see also the bilingual edition of H. Görgemanns and H. Karpp (Darmstadt, 1976), pp. 816–17. My translation follows H. U. von Balthasar, *Geist und Feuer*, 3d ed. (Einsiedeln and Freiburg, 1991), text 54, p. 67.

This inner connection between our idea of God and our picture of life beyond death is further demonstrated if we give even a brief glance to the history of religions. As far back as we can see in human history, the idea that everything ends with death has hardly ever existed. Some kind of idea of judgment and of survival can be found almost everywhere. But wherever the worldwide power of the one God has not yet been perceived, the picture of the other life remains vague and imprecise. It is an existence in nothingness, a shadowy mode of being, perceived as related in a remarkable way to the world of the living. On one hand, the spirits in the realm of shadow need the help of those still living to continue to survive; you have to feed them, look after them, in order to make it possible for them to be immortal even for a limited time. On the other hand, as spirits they have become powerful, members of the all-pervasive realm of spirits. They may be a threat or a help to men. People fear the return of spirits and use a variety of rituals to protect themselves from them. At the same time, it is the spirits of the ancestors, especially, who protect the clan and who are worshipped in order to be sure of their help. The ancestor-cult is one of the most primitive phenomena in tribal society; it gives expression to an awareness of human community that is unbroken even by death.

We would have to see the idea of reincarnation, which developed above all in Asian cultures, as being an attempt to explain the riddle of the injustice of this world in a nontheistic manner. In a painful existence, earlier wrongs are being atoned for, and thus, behind the seeming injustice of a world in which things go well for wrongdoers while the innocent suffer, becomes apparent the inflexible righteousness that ensures expiation for everything and puts everything straight. Yet when the whole of life in this world is experienced as suffering, such a transmigration of souls is no longer enough: the goal of all these purifications and transformations is then to escape from the bonds of individuality, from the whole confused cycle of existence, to sink down and to return to the original universal identity, which is at one and the same time nothing and everything.

It is certainly not by chance that today, with the fading of faith in the living God, all these archaic pictures are making a comeback, though of course they have lost their innocence and their moral dimension. Reincarnation, in which many people today once more believe, is no longer the means by which a hidden power of justice is at work, but rather a kind of extended application of the law of conservation of matter: the energy represented by the soul cannot merely disperse or disappear but each time requires some other embodiment. Nonetheless, the reappearance of this and other such views is an expression of man's inarticulate knowledge of the fact that death is not the last word in his existence; wherever we lose sight of the power of the living God, who will not let us fall, this dim knowledge finds expression in other and yet stranger fashions. Thus it gradually becomes clear what must happen for us to be able to say with conviction: I look for eternal life. We simply have to become once more aware of the living God and of his love. Then we will know that this love, which is eternal and is a great power, will not abandon us. But before we develop this idea in more detail and see how it picks up the individual fragments of human expectation, we have to turn once more to the difficulties of modern man, of what we ourselves are.

For, indeed, besides the main reason, the dying out of the idea of God, there are also other reasons for our difficulties with the hope of resurrection. In the first place, we are prevented from having a lively expectation of eternal life by being unable any longer to imagine anything of that kind. It may have been relatively easy, in earlier periods, to imagine heaven as a place of perfect beauty, joy, and peace. But the modern world view has mercilessly removed these aids to our imagination. But where there is no picture at all, the expectation evaporates as well, because human thought requires some kind of graphic form. Finally, there is the fact that an endless continuation of our existence does not actually seem desirable. It is already arduous enough; but even if everything went well, the idea of eternity appears to us like being condemned to boredom, as simply too much for man. Over against that, we would have to put the contrary question: Do we look for nothing more? If this were true, then the principle of hope, which Ernst Bloch posited as being the essence of Marxism, would not have been able to find so many supporters; then so many people would not have dedicated themselves to the faith in political utopias. A man who expects nothing is also unable to live any longer. Human existence, of its nature, stretches out into something greater.

But what do we actually expect? The primitive expectation within man, which cannot be taken away from him, finds expression in many and various ways. One of its most important manifestations is that we expect justice. We simply cannot come to terms with the idea of stronger people always winning the argument and being able to oppress the weaker ones; we cannot come to terms with the way that innocent people suffer, often in appalling fashion, and that all the luck in the world seems to drop into the laps of those who are guilty. The longing for justice, which has been so forcefully expressed in the struggles of those who have thought and suffered in every age, cannot be taken from us. We long for justice; and that is why we also long for truth. We see how lies spread out, impose themselves and that it becomes quite impossible to oppose them. We look for it not to continue that way, for the truth to be accorded its due. We long for senseless gossip, for cruelty and misery to come to an end; we long for the darkness of misunderstanding that divides us, our incapacity to love, to have an end and for true love to be really possible, freeing our life from its dungeon of loneliness, opening the door to others, opening the door to infinity without destroying us. We could even say: We long for true happiness. All of us.

2. What Is "Eternal Life"?

But that is exactly what is meant when we say "eternal life", which is not a matter of lasting a long time; rather, this expresses a certain quality of existence, in which duration, as an endless sequence of moments, disappears. That does of course mean that the longing for eternity becomes an act of defiance—defiance of eternity, a defiant assertion of finitude—whenever anyone is so identified with injustice, with lies, with hate, that the coming of justice, truth, and love would be a negation of his entire existence, so that he feels threatened by it at the inmost level of his being. Where there is such an existence, we have to describe it as damnation. Where lies and injustice have become the identifying characteristics of someone's life, then of course eternal life is the denial of this negative identity. Salvation becomes a punishment, because man has made a pact with destruction, and his whole life has fallen victim to negation.

After this glance at the ultimate danger to man, which positively demanded attention here, let us turn back to the positive side of things: Eternal life is not an endless sequence of moments, in which we would have to try to overcome boredom and anxiety in the face of what cannot be ended. Eternal life is a new quality of existence, in which everything flows together into the "now" of love, into that new quality of being that is freed from the fragmentation of existence in the accelerating flight of moments. In this, our mortal life, on one hand, every moment is too short, because life itself seems to pass away with the moment before we can catch hold of it; at the same time, each moment is too long for us, because the great number of moments, each always the same as the others, becomes too laborious for us. Thus it becomes clear that eternal life is not simply what comes afterward, something about which we can form no notion at all. Because it is a new quality of existence, it can be already present in the midst of this earthly life and its fleeting temporality as something new and different and greater, albeit in an imperfect and fragmentary fashion. But the dividing line between eternal and temporal life is by no means simply of a chronological order: so that the years before death would be temporal life; the endless time afterward would be eternal life—as we generally think. But because eternity is not just endless time but another level of being, such a merely chronological distinction cannot be right.

Eternal life is there, in the midst of time, wherever we come face to face with God; through the contemplation of the living God, it can become something like the firm base of our soul. Like a great love, it can no longer be taken from us by any change or chance; rather, it is an indestructible heart from which spring the courage and the joy to go on, even when exterior things are painful and hard. In Psalm 73 (72), we can see vividly how we should picture this, where, in the midst of the struggling and suffering of a believing man, that kind of experience breaks through in a flash and with quite stunning power. This psalm is the prayer of a man "who carries in his body anguish and illness"[3]—the prayer of a believer who has always made an attempt to live on the basis of the word of God but whose whole existence has now become pain and sheer contradiction.

The wisdom of the Old Covenant had formerly taught that God rewarded righteous dealing and punished wickedness. But the world in which the supplicant, the author of the prayer, is living mocks such notions: it is the experience of Job, that of Qoheleth, the experience of so many righteous men who have suffered under the Old Covenant, that finds expression here. Life seems to reward the cynics, those arrogant people who say: God takes no notice of what goes on here on earth. He does not respond. These people, who see themselves as gods, speak as if pronouncing from heaven, from the heights. The people eagerly accept their extravagant and superior-sounding words. They do not suffer. They are healthy and plump. They are unacquainted with life's troubles. The righteous man who is suffering is in danger of being confused. Does the world not show that the cynics are right? Maybe it really is senseless to stand by God and to live according to his justice? Perhaps he really does not respond to us? The solution occurs to the supplicant in the sanctuary, that is, when he turns in prayer to the living God and, in so doing, steps beyond the limits of purely private questioning and pondering. In entering the sanctuary he takes his place in the community of faith, among the signs of salvation, in the pilgrim company of God's history, and from that point of view he has a sight of God himself. And that changes his perspective. The way envy looks at the world becomes just as

[3] H.-J. Kraus, *Psalmen*, vol. 1 (Neukirchen and Vluyn, 1960), p. 506; for what follows, cf. the interpretation of the psalm by Kraus, pp. 503–11.

pointless as the crowing of pride. The illusory character of such good fortune becomes apparent; it dissolves like a dream upon waking, and the true perspective of reality re-emerges. "Nevertheless I am continually with you; you hold my right hand. You guide me with your counsel, and afterward you will receive me to glory. Whom have I in heaven but you? And there is nothing upon earth that I desire besides you. My flesh and my heart may fail, but God is the strength of my heart and my portion for ever. . . . For me it is good to be near God" (Ps 73:23–26, 28).

When God touches his soul man learns to see aright. Even if he had all possible possessions in heaven and earth, what would that be? The happiness of mere success, of mere power, of mere wealth, is always an illusory happiness; a glance at the world of today, looking into the tragedies of those powerful and successful people who have sold their souls for wealth, will show us how true this is. For those great fits of despair, against which all the refinements of desire and of its gratification are deployed in vain, do not occur among the poor and the weak but among those people who seem unacquainted with the troubles of life. Everything in heaven and on earth would be empty were it not for God, who has made himself our portion forever. "This is eternal life, that they know you the only true God, and Jesus Christ whom you have sent", says the Lord in the Gospel of John (17:3). This is exactly the discovery expressed in Psalm 73. The supplicant sees God and discovers that he needs nothing more, that in his contact with God everything has been granted him, true life. "Nothing in heaven or on earth gives me joy without you, even though my flesh should fail—my happiness is to be in your presence." Wherever such an encounter takes place, there is eternal life. The dividing line between temporal life and eternal life runs right through the midst of our temporal life. John distinguishes *bios*, as the passing life of this world, from *zoē*, as contact with the true life that wells up within us wherever we truly encounter God from within. This is what Jesus is saying in John's Gospel: "He who hears my word and believes him who sent me, has eternal life; he . . . has passed from death to life" (5:24). The saying from the story of Lazarus runs along the same lines: "I *am* the resurrection and the life; he who believes in me, though he die, yet shall he live, and whoever lives and believes in me shall never die" (Jn 11:25 [emphasis added]). The same experience is expressed in various ways in the letters of Paul, as for instance when Paul the prisoner, in chains, writes to the Philippians: "To me to live is Christ, and to die is gain." He would prefer to be released from the flesh and to be with Christ, but he recognizes that it is more important for him to remain for his congregations (Phil. 1:21–24). "If we live, we live to the Lord, and if we die, we die to the Lord; so then, whether we live or whether we die, we are the Lord's" (Rom 14:8).

3. "All That Is Mine Is Yours"

The Communal Aspect and the Presence Now of Eternal Life

Thus we see that eternal life is that mode of living, in the midst of our present earthly life, which is untouched by death because it reaches out beyond death. Eternal life in the midst of time, that is the first challenge of the article of belief that was our starting point. If we live in this way, then the hope of eternal fellowship with God will become the expectation that characterizes our existence, because some conception of its reality develops for us, and the beauty of it transforms us from within. Thus it becomes apparent that there is in this face-to-face encounter with God nothing selfish, no withdrawal into a merely private realm, but that very liberation from the self which alone makes any sense of eternity. An endless succession of moments would be unbearable; when our existence is gathered up into the single gaze of the love of God, this not only transforms endlessness into eternity, into God's today; at the same time it means fellowship with all those who have been accepted by that same love. In the kingdom of the Son of his love, as John Chrysostom once expressed it, there are no more "cold words [like] 'mine' and 'yours' ".[4] Because we all share in God's love, we belong to each other. Where God is all in all, we are all in everyone and all in ourselves, are in one Body, in the Body of Christ, in which the joy of one member is the joy of all other members, as the suffering of one member was the suffering of all members. That means two things:

a. Present and eternity are not, like present and future, located side by side and separated; rather, they are interwoven. That is the real difference between utopia and eschatology. For a long time, we have been offered utopia, that is, the hope of a better world in the future, in the place of eternal life. Eternal life is supposedly unreal; it is said to alienate us from real time. But utopia is a real goal toward which we can work with all our powers and abilities. Yet this idea is a misapprehension that leads us to the destruction of our hopes. For this future world, for the sake of which the present is being used up, never comes to us ourselves; it is always only there for some future generation, as yet unknown. It is like the water and the fruit that are offered to Tantalus: the water always reaches just up to his neck, and

[4] Von Balthasar, "Mensch", p. 11.

the fruit is always just in front of his mouth. But when, in his great thirst, he wants to drink, the water withdraws beyond his reach, and when he wants to taste the fruit, in his hunger, the same thing happens. This ancient picture of the damnation of pride, as the most typical sin of man, pinpoints exactly that hubris which replaces eschatology with self-made utopia, that is to say that it intends to fulfill man's hope by its own powers and without faith in God. Utopia always seems quite close but never arrives because man always remains free and can therefore never be fixed in place in a final state of things. The struggle to keep evil under control, within limits, has to be taken up anew by each generation and can never be removed by the institutional arrangements of an earlier generation.

Maintaining that there is an inner logic in history, which will necessarily result in the emergence of the just society in the end (that is to say, will therefore produce different people) is a primitive myth that aims at replacing the idea of God with that of an anonymous power; believing in this is in no sense enlightened but simply illogical. Belief in utopia has been able to replace the hope of eternal life to such a great extent in the modern world because it fulfilled the two basic conditions for being modern: it concerned something we make ourselves, which has no need of a transcendent God (though of course it does require a divine immanent logic of history). Because it concerns something artificial, this future world is also conceivable: always as close as Tantalus' fruit and always just as far away. We should finally bid farewell to the notion of working to build the ideal society of the future as being a myth and should instead work with total commitment to strengthen those factors that hold evil at bay in the present and that can therefore offer some guarantee for the immediate future.

b. But that happens at the very moment when eternal life becomes effective in the midst of time. For that means that God's will is done "on earth, as it is in heaven". Earth becomes heaven, becomes the Kingdom of God, whenever God's will is done there as in heaven. We pray for this because we know that it does not lie within our power to draw heaven down here. For the Kingdom of God is *his* Kingdom, not our kingdom, not within our sway; because it is so, it is final and can be relied upon. But it is always quite near wherever God's will is accepted. For that is where truth springs up, justice arises, love comes to be. The Kingdom of God is much closer than the Tantalus-fruit of utopia because it is not a chronological future, does not come chronologically later, but refers at all times to the wholly other, which for that very reason is able to embed itself within time, so as simply to take it up within itself and make of it pure presence. Eternal life, which takes its beginning in communion with God here and now, seizes this here and now and takes it up within the great expanse of true reality, which is no longer fragmented by the stream of time. There, the mutual impermeability of I and thou can no longer exist, as this is closely associated with the fragmentation of time. In fact, anyone who sets his will within the will of God deposits it right there, where all good will has its place; and thus our will blends with the will of all others. Wherever this happens, the saying becomes true: I live, and yet no longer I—Christ lives in me. The mystery of Christ, who is, as Origen beautifully expresses it, the Kingdom of God in person, is the determinative center for the understanding of eternal life.

Before we follow up this idea a little further, I would like to offer one final reference to the realism of the Christian hope in the wholly other, in God's eternal Kingdom. How strongly belief in eternal life can take effect in the midst of the present time may be seen perhaps more impressively than anywhere else in the writings of Augustine, who had to live through the collapse of the Roman empire and of all its civilizing institutions, that is to say, a period of history full of troubles and horrors. But he knew, and he could see, that a new city was springing up, the city of God. When he talks about this, one can feel how he is inwardly warmed: "When death has been swallowed up in victory, then these things will be no more; and there will be peace—perfect and eternal peace. We will be in a kind of city. Brothers, when I speak of this city, even though the troubles here grow great, I can no longer contain myself."[5] The future city is a support to him because in certain respects it is a city that is already present— wherever the Lord brings us together in his Body and places our wills within the will of God.

Life shared with God, eternal life within temporal life, is possible because of God's living with us: Christ is God being here with us. In him God has time for us; he is God's time for us and thus at the same time the opening of time into eternity. God is no longer the distant and indeterminate God to whom no bridge will reach; he is the God at hand: the Body of the Son is the bridge for our souls. Through him, each single person's relationship with God has been blended together in his one relationship with God, so that turning one's gaze toward God is no longer a matter of turning one's gaze away from others and from the world, but a uniting of our gaze and of our being with the single gaze and the one being of the Son. Because he has descended right to the depths of the earth (Eph 4:9f.), God is no longer merely a God up there, but God surrounds us from above, from below, and from within: he is all in all, and therefore all in all belongs to

---

[5] *Enarratio in Ps.* 84:10, CCL 39:1170; cf. P. Brown, *Augustine of Hippo* (Berkeley: University of California Press, 1967), pp. 299–312.

us: "All that is mine is yours." God's being "all in all" began with Christ's renunciation on the Cross of what was properly his. It will be complete when the Son finally hands over to the Father the Kingdom, that is, ingathered humanity and the creation that is carried with them (1 Cor 15:28).

That is why the purely private existence of the isolated self no longer exists, but "all that is mine is yours." This glorious declaration of the Father to the rebellious son (Lk 15:31), which Jesus then used to describe his own relationship to the Father in his high-priestly prayer (Jn 17:10), is true also in the Body of Christ for all of us with each other. Each accepted pain, no matter how obscure, every silent suffering of evil, each act of inwardly overcoming oneself, every outreach of love, each renunciation, and every turning in silence to God—all of that now becomes effective as a whole: Nothing that is good goes for nothing. Against the power of evil, whose tentacles threaten to surround and lay hold of every part of our society, to choke it in their deadly embrace, this quiet cycle of true life appears as the liberating force by which the Kingdom of God, without any abolition of what is existing, is, as the Lord says, already in the midst of us (Lk 17:21). Within this cycle God's Kingdom comes, because God's will is done on earth as in heaven.

4. Particular Questions concerning Christian Eschatology

All of this has now outlined the main features of what our faith means by the words "heaven" and "hell".[6] The meaning of the "place of purification" can likewise be easily

---

[6] For supporting arguments and demonstration, and for further details, I refer you to my book *Eschatologie*, 6th ed. (Regensburg, 1990).

understood on this basis. Ultimately, the place of purification is Christ himself. When we encounter him without disguise, then as a matter of course everything that is wretched and guilty in our lives, which we have for the most part kept carefully hidden, in that moment of truth will stand before our soul in flames of fire. The effect of the presence of the Lord upon everything within us that is interwoven with injustice, with hate, and with lies will be as a burning flame. It will become a purifying pain, which will burn away from within us everything that cannot be reconciled with eternity, with the living cycle of Christ's love.

And we can understand the meaning of judgment on this same basis. Here again, we can say that Christ himself is the judgment, he who is truth and love personified. He came into this world as the inner standard and measure for each individual life. The fact that he who became incarnate, the crucified and risen One, is himself the judgment involves two interconnected aspects. First of all, this implies what we were just considering: Everything base, twisted, and sinful in our existence will be exposed by this standard; we have to be freed from it in the pain of purification. But there is also a second aspect. Romano Guardini, who in his inclination to melancholy often felt the dreadful and painful aspects of this world most grievously, like a burden laid upon him personally, said many times that he knew that at the judgment God would ask him about his life. But he was waiting for the judgment to be able for his part to put questions to God—the question about why creation exists, about all the incomprehensible things that have arisen in it as the consequence of the freedom to do evil. The judgment means that God puts this question to himself. Hans Urs von Balthasar expresses it this way: Those who defend God are not convincing; God has to defend himself. "He did it once, when the Risen One

showed his wounds . . . . God himself has to invent his theo-
dicy. He must already have worked it out when he endowed
men with the freedom (and thus with the temptation) to say
No to him, to his commands." [7] At the judgment, in response
to our questions, the Lord will show us his wounds, and we
will understand. In the meantime, however, he simply expects us to stand by him and to believe what these wounds tell
us, even though we cannot work right through the logic of
this world.

One last question remains: What about the soul? And: Should
we expect a real resurrection, a bodily resurrection of the
dead, and a new world? In the past twenty-five years, the
word "soul" has very widely been placed on the list of for-
bidden words; people try to talk around it wherever possible.
People have tried to persuade us that this is a pagan (Greek)
conception, which could have no place in Christian thinking,
because this depicts the splitting up of the human being, it is
said, in a way that cannot be reconciled with the unity of the
Creator and of his creation. Both of these are untrue. The
word "soul" is to be found in all cultures, with basic mean-
ings that are related but that developed in very varied fashion
in individual instances. In the way it is used in the Christian
tradition, it is a product of faith, impossible to conceive outside the context of the gospel of Jesus Christ and in fact
appearing nowhere else. It expresses the particular character
of the human being, as intended by the Creator: man is that
creature in which spirit and material meet together and are
united in a single whole. If we set aside the word "soul", then
we inevitably fall into a materialistic conception in which the
body is not exalted but robbed of its dignity. When many

[7] Balthasar, "Mensch", p. 9.

people say that a disembodied soul, between death and resurrection, is an absurdity, then obviously they have not listened carefully enough to Holy Scripture. For since the Ascension of Christ the problem of the soul's being disembodied no longer exists: the Body of Christ is the new heaven, which is no longer closed. If we ourselves have become members of the Body of Christ, then our souls are safely held within this body, which has become *their* body, and thus they await the final resurrection, in which God will be all in all.

But this resurrection at the end of history is something truly new. We cannot imagine it, because we are ignorant both of the possibilities of the material and of the capacities of the Creator. Yet we do know, since the Resurrection of Christ, not only that individuals will be saved, but that God intends to save his entire creation and that he is able to do this. Creation, which was thrown down by Adam and which is being trampled upon by him ever anew and ever more thoroughly, is waiting for the children of God. Where they are, the creation is also renewed. I would like to close with a quotation from a sermon by Augustine, which seems to me to make marvelously clear the basic drift of what is meant by the expectation of eternal life in the midst of the present life: "A girl may perhaps say to her beloved: 'Don't wear this cloak', and he doesn't wear it. If she says to him in winter, 'I like you best in a short tunic', then he will prefer to freeze rather than upset her. Yet, surely, she has no power to punish him? . . . No, there is just one thing he fears: 'Otherwise, I will never see you again.' " [8] This is what looking forward to eternal life means: not wanting to be lost from the sight of God, because he is our life.

---

[8] *Sermo* 161:10. Cf. Brown, *Augustine*, p. 215.

List of Sources

GOD WITH US AND GOD AMONG US
"By the Power of the Holy Spirit He Was Born
of the Virgin Mary, and Became Man"
    Published, under the title "Et incarnatus est de Spiritu Sancto ex Maria
Virgine", in *30 Tage in Kirche und Welt* 5 (1995), no. 4, pp. 59–67; and in
Klerusblatt 75 (1995): 107–10.

GOD'S YES AND HIS LOVE ARE MAINTAINED EVEN IN DEATH
The Origin of the Eucharist in the Paschal Mystery
    Eucharistie—Mitte der Kirche (Munich, 1978), pp. 9–20, 67f. *

---

* The Preface reads:

    In the crisis of faith we are presently experiencing, it is again and again
the correct celebration and the right understanding of the Eucharist that
prove to be at the center of the debate. That is why I was happy to use the
four Lenten sermons that Father Wagner, S.J., of Saint Michael's Church, in
Munich, invited me to deliver in order to develop some basic teaching
about this sacrament, in which I could go into the main problems of
liturgical form, and of liturgical reform, and likewise into the central questions of dogma. To that extent, the particular emphases here are simply
determined by the situation of the time; I hope, nevertheless, that none of
the basic themes of Catholic teaching on the Eucharist has been entirely
overlooked.

    The text published here is based on that taken down from a tape record-
ing of the sermons, and I must express my heartfelt thanks to the Press
Office of the Archdiocese of Munich for their care in recording and tran-
scribing it. I have smoothed out the vocabulary and style for publication and
also added just a little here and there, but I have deliberately left unchanged
the basic flavor of the spoken word. Thus, it goes without saying that this is
not a scholarly treatment of the subject but in fact adult catechesis, which is,
certainly, based on repeated scholarly study of the basic material. The notes
are therefore restricted to giving details of works directly referred to in the
text; there is no intention of opening up any wider scholarly discussion.
Thus, the sole aim of this little book is to point out, for the purposes of

----

teaching the faith and also for reflection on one's personal faith, the basic
benchmarks offered to us by the faith of the Church down through the ages.
I hope in this way to offer a modest degree of help to all those who are
struggling to achieve a contemporary expression of the faith in our time.

Presently in Rome, on the Feast of the Assumption, 1978
Joseph Cardinal Ratzinger

STANDING BEFORE THE LORD—
WALKING WITH THE LORD—
KNEELING BEFORE THE LORD
Celebrating Corpus Christi

> Sermon for the Feast of Corpus Christi on May 25, 1978, on the Marienplatz. Published in *Ordinariats-Korrespondenz* 03–14/1978, of June 1, 1978, no. 19, pp. 1–4.

WE WHO ARE MANY ARE ONE BODY, ONE BREAD
(1 Corinthians 10:17)
Eucharist and the Church

> The first section is taken from notes of the lecture "The Doctrine of the Eucharist" (summer session, 1963), which were copied in manuscript form, pp. 74ff.
>
> The second section is an extract from the first pastoral letter of the Archbishop of Freising and Munich, dated June 19, 1977, and published in *Ordinariats-Korrespondenz* 03–8/77.

PEACE FROM THE LORD
"Peace" as One of the Names of the Eucharistic Sacrament

> The first section is an extract from the sermon preached on December 3, 1978, in the Cathedral of Our Lady, Munich, on the occasion of the seventieth birthday of Ernst Tewes.
>
> The second section is an extract from the New Year's Eve sermon of 1981.

A CHURCH OF ALL TIMES AND PLACES
Celebrating in Communion with the Pope

> The sermon for Papal Sunday, July 10, 1977, in St. Michael's Church in Munich, published in *Ordinariats-Korrespondenz* 03–10/77.

THE CHURCH SUBSISTS AS LITURGY AND IN THE LITURGY
A Homily on Acts 2:42

> Sermon of the Archbishop of Munich and Freising, Joseph Cardinal Ratzinger, on the occasion of the ordination of priests in the Cathedral of St. Mary, Freising, on June 28, 1980; published in *Ordinariats-Korrespondenz* 03–10/80, of July 2, 1980, no. 26.

MY JOY IS TO BE IN THY PRESENCE
On the Christian Belief in Eternal Life

Lecture to the Christian Academy in Prague, March 30, 1992. Published under the title: "Daß Gott Alles in Allem sei, Vom christlichen Glauben an das ewige Leben" ["That God may be all in all": Concerning the Christian belief in eternal life], in *Klerusblatt* 72 (1992): 203–7.